ONE SIGNAL
PUBLISHERS

ATRIA

BLOOD MONEY

The Story of Life, Death, and Profit
Inside America's Blood Industry

KATHLEEN McLAUGHLIN

ONE SIGNAL
PUBLISHERS
—
ATRIA
New York London Toronto Sydney New Delhi

An Imprint of Simon & Schuster, Inc.
1230 Avenue of the Americas
New York, NY 10020

Certain names and characteristics have been changed.

A portion of the prologue was adapted from an essay by the author
first published by the *Guardian* (2018).

First One Signal Publishers/Atria Books hardcover edition January 2023

ONE SIGNAL PUBLISHERS / ATRIA BOOKS and colophon are trademarks
of Simon & Schuster, Inc.

For information about special discounts for bulk purchases,
please contact Simon & Schuster Special Sales at 1-866-506-1949 or
business@simonandschuster.com.

The Simon & Schuster Speakers Bureau can bring authors to your live event.
For more information or to book an event, contact the
Simon & Schuster Speakers Bureau at 1-866-248-3049 or visit our website
at www.simonspeakers.com.

Interior design by Lexy East

Manufactured in the United States of America

1   3   5   7   9   10   8   6   4   2

Library of Congress Cataloging-in-Publication Data

Names: McLaughlin, Kathleen (Journalist), author.
Title: Blood money : the story of life, death, and profit inside America's blood industry /
by Kathleen McLaughlin.
Description: First One Signal Publishers/Atria Books hardcover edition. |
New York : One Signal Publishers/Atria, 2023. | Includes index.
Identifiers: LCCN 2022034219 (print) | LCCN 2022034220 (ebook) |
ISBN 9781982171964 (hardcover) | ISBN 9781982171971 (paperback) |
ISBN 9781982171988 (ebook)
Subjects: LCSH: Blood banks—United States. | Blood products—United States.
Classification: LCC RM172 .M39 2023 (print) | LCC RM172 (ebook) |
DDC 362.17/840973—dc23/eng/20220929
LC record available at https://lccn.loc.gov/2022034219
LC ebook record available at https://lccn.loc.gov/2022034220

ISBN 978-1-9821-7196-4
ISBN 978-1-9821-7198-8 (ebook)

For Wang Shuping and Gao Yaojie

Blind to their suffering, deaf to their sharp words,
The gully of greed can never be filled.

—Gao Yaojie

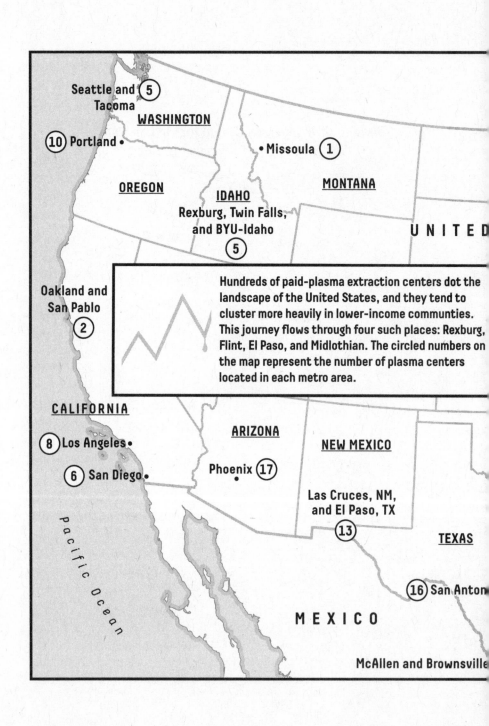

Seattle and Tacoma (5)

WASHINGTON

(10) Portland •

• Missoula (1)

OREGON

MONTANA

IDAHO
Rexburg, Twin Falls,
and BYU-Idaho
(5)

UNITED

Oakland and
San Pablo
(2)

Hundreds of paid-plasma extraction centers dot the landscape of the United States, and they tend to cluster more heavily in lower-income communties. This journey flows through four such places: Rexburg, Flint, El Paso, and Midlothian. The circled numbers on the map represent the number of plasma centers located in each metro area.

CALIFORNIA

ARIZONA

NEW MEXICO

(8) Los Angeles •

Phoenix (17)
•

(6) San Diego •

Las Cruces, NM,
and El Paso, TX
(13)

TEXAS

Pacific Ocean

(16) San Anton

MEXICO

McAllen and Brownsville

CONTENTS

PROLOGUE
Smuggling Blood

I plunged into the world of international smuggling with the stroke of a pen.

It was 2004 in Shanghai, and I had just told the first of many lies about the contents of my luggage. I had concealed in my suitcases a dozen glass vials of medication made from human blood, extracted from people living elsewhere in the world. The Chinese government had banned exactly this—imported blood and products made from blood—decades earlier, in the midst of a deadly crisis borne partly in human blood.

The corridors of Shanghai Pudong International Airport, a polished, shining colossus of marble walkways, metal beams, and glass walls, stood tall, in stark contrast to the low-rent soft-sided lunch coolers slung over each of my shoulders. I trudged through long, crowded halls to the customs inspection station. When my turn came, I handed a stern, formal agent in a black cap my papers. The first was a small, boxy entry card with my name and other personal details. The second was longer—a customs entry document with a series of detailed questions about the contents of my luggage. Despite all the detailed documents required, those bags were never physically inspected.

In the dozens of times I traveled in and out of China, my bags were never searched by anyone—something I would depend on. Seeing my check in the "no" column to a question about carrying human blood, the agent stamped my U.S. passport and I was free to go. I walked back into the country where I worked and lived: China. It was that easy to start smuggling blood, and simple to continue doing it for years.

Back home in the United States a day earlier, I had gently packed the clear, breakable glass vials into my purple picnic coolers. Half the vials contained a syrupy liquid; the other half held dried white nuggets made of human immune particles extracted from blood plasma. I tucked the glass bottles inside soft clothes and socks, a little insurance against them being broken in the baggage hold. Days or weeks later, when I finally needed it, a white-uniformed nurse in a Shanghai hospital would mix the solids with the liquids, then infuse the resulting syrup into my vein. Before that, I had to move these vials, along with my own vein catheter needles, IV bags, and tubing lines, to the other side of the world. I knew I was breaking the law, but it didn't seem like that big of a deal.

I moved to Shanghai for a magazine job in the early 2000s, only months after learning I had a rare immune disease that would demand regular treatment with a medicine made from human blood plasma. My condition had begun to break down my body, and while the decision seems wildly irrational looking back on it, I remember how excited I was to settle in somewhere that felt far from the States' cultural stigmas about illness and disability. In China, I had the privilege of living as an outsider; I could pretend to be normal and healthy. People there didn't know my personal business the same way they might back home. But my new base was far from perfect. The fact that I needed to smuggle blood illustrated the problems in its health-care system. At that time, China was still grappling with an AIDS epidemic from a decade earlier, fueled in part by its blood trade. Covering up the outbreak had made it much worse than it might have been.

With good reason, China banned blood imports from the rest of the world in 1985. The virus that causes AIDS had spread fast, and blood was the culprit in thousands of cases around the globe. Just as the AIDS crisis peaked in the mid-1980s and scientists discovered the virus that causes the disease is transmitted in blood, six global drug companies were accused of selling HIV-tainted blood products in a series of lawsuits that were eventually settled. Thousands of hemophiliacs around the world had been infected via tainted blood products that came from the United States.

China's ban on foreign blood helped it keep the disease from arriving in the country in a large wave through medicines as it had elsewhere. Yet the government's persistent lie that AIDS was a "foreign disease"—an offshoot of Western social ills like prostitution, homosexuality, and promiscuity, all of which of course existed in China, despite the government's denials—created the perfect conditions in that country for a homegrown epidemic. China's government knew HIV was a risk for blood and plasma donors, but it insisted on downplaying any potential risk within the domestic system and resisted giving donors a way to protect themselves from potential threat. Thousands unwittingly took the disease home to their families, or spread it through blood donations, the victims sometimes left to die without ever knowing what it was that was killing them.

In the 1990s, the virus ripped through parts of the country, with much of the then-deadly virus spread by China's domestic trade in human blood plasma. In those days, the United States had broader access to lifesaving medication for AIDS, but the situation was different, and more dangerous, in other parts of the world. When I was reporting on the disease in southwestern China in 2007, I learned that only 3 percent of Chinese nationals with HIV had access to the antiretroviral drugs that would save their lives, even though there was a government program that paid for them. While the illness was survivable for many people in wealthier countries, China was still a place where essential AIDS medications weren't easy to come by.

Although the government had made an effort to clean the system up, the human blood supply chain remained unsafe when I moved to Shanghai. Stories of HIV and hepatitis infections carried through commercial blood and plasma supplies appeared every so often in the news, and it felt like danger lurked in every vial. Corruption in the health-care sector led to cutting corners on safety protocols like blood testing and sterile equipment. Heat treatment had rendered the medicines made from blood plasma safer in the United States by this time, but it was still spotty in China. Knowing all this, for most of my fifteen years in China, I maintained personal access to a safe blood supply with frequent trips back to the United States. It kept my condition under control.

For years without interruption, I moved other people's blood particles across the Pacific Ocean in my suitcases. When one hospital grew a little leery of our arrangement, I'd move to a new doctor in Shanghai or Beijing who would agree to bend the rules a little bit and infuse the drugs I'd brought from abroad. They would also stop after a few months or years, when someone on staff complained (probably rightly so) about the unusual accommodation. The rules were more flexible then; I don't think I'd be able to get away with any of this now. By the time I left China in 2016, the political environment had worsened. The government's authoritarian hand has grown much heavier, and legal gray areas narrowed significantly. I haven't tried to return to China since I disclosed my blood-smuggling secret in a piece for an international newspaper in 2019, but years of reporting on labor and politics had already put me on thin ice with the country's government. I have no idea if I would be allowed back again.

When I told the lie about my luggage on the customs form, I reasoned that the bottles were just medication, a proprietary mix of extremely expensive chemicals. I had, twice before, tried to ship the vials through proper channels, with no success. Customs agents in Shanghai decided the $20,000 declared value was so high that I must be planning to start a clinic, and therefore the importation should be taxed as such. After three days of my pleading with agents and promising I'd never to do it again, the officers let me pick up the medication without a fine. After that, I decided it was easier to go underground than to try to play by the rules.

Bringing fragments of other people's blood into the country didn't concern me much, odd as that may sound. For that to make sense, I first need to explain what China was like in the 2000s, when I lived there. Xi Jinping's security and surveillance apparatus had not yet tightly gripped the country. Many forbidden endeavors that seem obvious now were allowed to exist in the legal shadows and corners. Though the government was unmistakably authoritarian before Xi took power, the country's political leaders throughout the 2000s were experimenting with more openness than China had seen in generations. The frenzy of new possibilities was especially evident on its frontiers. No country has more miles of international borders than China. In the 2000s and early 2010s, those boundaries were porous; in some places, they were nearly undetectable. Smugglers moved back and forth across the lines as a matter of routine. The rules were even more flexible for those who traveled to and from the country on business.

In those days, nobody checked my bags coming in or going out—anywhere, it seemed. In rural, remote reaches, a bustling cross-border trade regularly flouted checkpoints, taxes, and laws. While out on reporting trips to the borders with Myanmar, North Korea, and Vietnam, I saw smugglers scale fences and steer boats across rivers in broad daylight, carrying bags and boxes of clothes, rice, fish, cooking oil, booze, and full of other contents unknown. I met women who had been tricked into coming to China illegally for what they thought were housekeeping or cooking jobs and who often ended up as unwilling brides for sale and sex workers, trafficked within the country's borders by human smugglers. But then, I was operating on a much smaller scale, with a smuggling practice that didn't affect anyone but me. I could, and so many times did, go to hospitals in Shanghai and Beijing with bottles of smuggled medication and ask the staff to inject the liquid into my vein.

Even though I created my own small place in the smuggling world, the magnitude of this underground economy at that time felt staggering to me. When American-style bejeweled engagement rings caught on in China, diamond smugglers filled the gap. Young couples who wanted to buy wedding adornments were hit with a prohibitively expensive luxury tax when the stones were imported through proper channels. The solution? For a short period in the late 2000s, most diamonds sold in China were smuggled into the country, mostly in brokers' suitcases.

Similarly, the fruits of the U.S. entertainment industry were pirated and smuggled to such an extent that in China, we often watched blockbusters on bootleg DVDs at the same time as they were released in the States, sometimes even before.

Even one of America's most senior trade officials engaged in the game. In 1998, while negotiating China's entry into the World Trade Organization, President Clinton's top trade representative, Charlene Barshefsky, was busted bringing too many Beanie Babies into the United States on her way home. In my case, the illicit, smuggled goods were not for kicks or profit.

The Plasma Economy

By the time I got to China in the early 2000s, the factories that make the world's things were rapidly becoming China's fastest highway to wealth. Just twenty years before, this had been a poor country, laying the groundwork for a new, more open economic structure, erecting the epic workshops and production lines that would thrust the country to world economic and political power. By the 1990s, whole regions started organizing around mass-producing single products. I reported on a village nicknamed "Bra Town," because that's what they made.

Were it not for the deadly viral bombs buried in the supply chain, the appropriately bizarre blood plasma economy of rural Henan, one of the most populous parts of the country, might have been just another clever nickname for a plot to derive wealth from whatever raw resource was most plentiful. Rural Chinese people sought and sometimes lost fortunes on schemes small and large, like ant farms, stone carving, brewing liquor, and building the world's toys and clothes. The possibilities seemed ever limitless, and in Henan one thing everyone had to sell was their own plasma—the watery, yellowish protein component of blood.

For some Chinese urbanites, Henan remains a joke, much like elitist Americans on the coasts like to mock West Virginia or Idaho. The origins of that mockery are likewise based on flawed ideas about wealth and class. The stereotypes persist.

When China began to open up its economy, officials in Henan started the plasma business. The region's farmers, for generations captive to poverty, could make money by selling their blood protein in government-managed clinics that would whirl their fluids into medicines and profits. The blood-centered scheme would create wealth while sheltering China's people from the dangers of imports of the kind that scandalized and sickened people in Japan, Hong Kong, and other places. The blood trade created wealth in a part of the country where the most abundant natural resource was human bodies.

China embraced warp-speed growth with its own version of capitalism, and its citizens grabbed onto whatever notions might make them rich. If that meant selling blood—the essence of life—the farmers would sell blood. In his *Dream of Ding Village*, a fictionalized tale about the Henan plasma economy disaster, the Chinese writer Yan

Lianke describes life in a community thriving, then crumpling, on its blood economy. The business left an iron-rich scent in the air. This odor was not invented. Yan spent months investigating the trade, and the villagers told him about the ubiquitous smell of blood across the region in the mid-1990s. He wrote:

> The grass upon the plain has turned brittle and dry. The trees are all bare; the crops have withered. The villagers are shrunken inside their homes, never to emerge again.
> Ever since the blood came. Ever since the blood ran red.

Yan writes fiction, but in the hands of contemporary Chinese writers, the genre is a somewhat tolerated technique to reveal the truth. His blood novel reads like poetry, based on extensive work in his native province listening to the stories of blood sellers and their fates. After it was published, I met him over dinner in Beijing, in an American cowboy-themed restaurant he chose, and he spun more tales of the plasma economy. It sounded like a dark, twisted novel. It was reality.

———

In Henan, what began as the promise of wealth morphed into certain pain and death. It infiltrated and annihilated entire communities, leaving behind orphans and dire poverty, much of it covered up by local and provincial governments. This province became ground zero for the AIDS outbreak within China, driven by the blood plasma economy. Years after the initial bomb, still-unknown numbers of people in the region lived with HIV infections they got through selling their blood plasma. They were lucky to be alive but dependent on government generosity to pay for their medications and living costs. One of the men whose blood was extracted as raw material in the reckless days of China's plasma economy told me what it had done to his life and his village. Decades after it happened, speaking to a foreign journalist was still a risky endeavor, but especially to do so back in Henan. Instead, we met hundreds of miles away.

He and other survivors of the catastrophe that hit his village still lived under heavy surveillance, so I could not travel to their homes to learn what happened. Instead, I waited until one December, when a group of AIDS patients and their family members made their annual 450-mile trek to the Chinese capital for a protest on World AIDS Day. They were usually allowed to mull around outside the massive government health building for a while before the police ushered them back onto trains that would return them home to their faraway towns. The protesters let officials know they were still living and still angry at what had befallen them. Their efforts rarely resulted in anything concrete, but sometimes the government raised the amount of compensation it paid to victims of the infection. I sat in the back seat of a cab, a couple of blocks from the protest, while the protester, a slight figure in a lightweight blue jacket, stood outside my open car door. We spoke to each other while facing in opposite directions, hoping nobody saw us chatting.

He had worked as a farmer, one of the people in China who toiled the hardest for the least money. During the blood rush, he could sell his blood for $8 for a half liter once every second or third day. It was a simple, almost ridiculously easy way to make good money— something none of the villagers had been able to find before. It was impossible to resist. People in his village built new homes, bought cars, ate better meals, and life seemed to be on the way up. The man sold his plasma for several years and accumulated a small savings.

Then the government suddenly shut down all the blood stations without telling the plasma sellers why. There was no warning about an AIDS risk, no explanation for the abrupt closures. The quick cash disappeared and few knew about the deadly viral land mines left behind. A few years later, people in this man's village began falling ill and dying early, in agony. He had heard of AIDS. He believed the government's assurances that it was a foreign disease that Chinese people wouldn't get. Then a doctor diagnosed him with it. About one-quarter of roughly 2,000 people in his village sold blood plasma. By the time I met him, more than 200 of his friends, neighbors, and family members—a full one-tenth of the village's population—had died from complications of AIDS, he told me.

The virus left his body so weak that he had trouble working the way he had before. The meager compensation he received from the government for having been made sick wasn't enough to get by in what was becoming an ever more expensive country. But still, he was one of the lucky—someone who lived to tell his story. Each year he and his cohorts took the train back to Beijing to protest, and each year they went home with nothing but the satisfaction of having made their presence known.

By most widely accepted estimates, roughly 1 million people were infected with HIV as a result of the provincial government's pay-for-plasma system. The exact number, including the true number of people who died due to the scandal, remains a secret carefully buried and guarded by the Chinese government. If not for two women—both doctors, but from different eras—who exposed the crisis, the death and devastation would have been much worse. One discovered the epidemic; the other became a cherished public figure insisting it be acknowledged. Without the work of these women, I wouldn't have smuggled my own blood products into China. Like most Chinese people at that time, I would have been exposed to a wildly unsafe medical system, the traces of which still threaten patients and donors today. As of 2009, AIDS had become the leading cause of death in China among infectious diseases.

By the time I moved to China in 2002, the government wanted people to believe the epidemic was under control and blood supplies were safe. People I met over the years told a different story. I once interviewed a group of men who contracted a rare neurological illness after a chemical exposure cluster in northern China. They used the same medication I do, made from human blood plasma. When I asked if they knew about the HIV risk, they nodded and said, "Of course." They talked about it all the time; they were always worried about it. They even had to sign a waiver acknowledging the potential risk. But what else could they do? They didn't have imported or smuggled medicines like I did.

The Warnings

Drs. Gao Yaojie and Wang Shuping were strangers with no ties except location until the AIDS scandal emerged in the 1990s. By then, Dr. Gao had retired. She was a gynecologist who still did public health work education, teaching sex workers and youth about safer sex practices. Dr. Wang was a medical researcher studying blood-borne viruses. I visited Gao Yaojie four times in New York, where she lived in exile, today well into her nineties. She escaped to America late in life, under threat of imprisonment or worse. Gao never learned to speak English, so she connected to the world online and only in Chinese. She became well known as a crusader, nicknamed back home in China as the "AIDS Granny."

When we first met in 2013, Dr. Gao was a tiny woman, her health under strain from illness and the stress of having fled alone to an unfamiliar country. Her feet were bound for a time when she was young, but the bandages were removed when the practice fell out of favor later in her life. As a result, she walked with a bit of a limp. She had a personality that filled the room, however, and an authoritative way of speaking, loudly. She also had a real temper—the perfect personality to publicly take on one of the world's most secretive governments over a crisis it had helped create and didn't want to deal with.

I turned up at her apartment in West Harlem, New York City, to try to piece together what had happened in Henan. For me, it was as much a personal mission as a journalistic one. I had been captivated by the AIDS crisis and subsequent cover-up in China, and also by its origins, given how I relied on one of the key medications whose source was responsible for the crisis. When I met Gao, she lived in a large complex that had become a low-income housing fortress complete with guards, cameras, and multiple locks. I've often thought back to that first meeting, chuckling that perhaps the most powerful person in the building at that time was a little Chinese grandmother.

In that first conversation, Gao told me she left China with only a blood-pressure cuff and a portable hard drive that preserved a thousand photos of victims of the epidemic. Before she agreed to talk with me, she sent me a list of rules. She would not discuss China's politics, its political leaders, or the general topic of dissidents. She was wary of being portrayed as an all-purpose politics critic. I didn't blame her at all. Her focus was the AIDS epidemic and cover-up.

As I got to know her, I saw Dr. Gao as eccentric, kind, and entertaining, but prone to dark moods. Who wouldn't be, living in exile?

She spent most of her time bedridden, writing and researching, and reliving memories of what she had seen in China, in a lifetime that spanned eras of political turmoil. Across the days and months, she emailed contacts back home and added to her writing. When we first met, she was putting the last touches on her twenty-seventh book, the ninth to chronicle China's AIDS epidemic. In the years after, she kept writing.

"You wouldn't understand the earlier books; they were too technical," she told me for a 2013 profile in *BuzzFeed*. I laughed, but I could tell right away she was not someone I wanted to argue with. Seventeen years before, just after she retired as a gynecologist and professor at a medical school in her home province, Gao was such a thorn in the side of the government that she had to escape to the United States. She eventually fled China with the aid of Hillary Clinton, then the U.S. secretary of state.

"I didn't do this because I wanted to become involved in politics," she said back then. "I just saw that the AIDS patients were so miserable. They were so miserable."

As we spoke, Gao began to reveal horror stories. She spoke of young men and women, the poorest in the province, caught up in plasma fervor. The blood rush was so intense that people went to the extraction centers as often as they could. There were wild rumors of a man who stood on his head to keep his blood flowing so he could sell more of his fluid. The people of Henan got just a drop for their plasma, while go-betweens amassed personal profits selling what they advertised as a pure supply. Villages were littered with bright red slogans and banners: "Stick out an arm, show a vein, open your hand, and make a fist, 50 kuai" (at the time, about $6). "If you want a comfortable standard of living, go sell your plasma." "To give plasma is an honor."

First it was a frenzy, and then, in a few years, the sickness and death replaced the giddiness. Gao's first patient confirmed with AIDS was a young woman who never got better after giving birth. The woman died soon after her child was born. Stories of death and tragedy seemed endless. Gao told them to whoever would listen. She wrote books and poems, gave speeches, and angered local officials and the power far off in Beijing. Her writing from that era was as cutting as her press interviews:

Like a vampire, you have the people's blood on your hands.
Blind to their suffering, deaf to their sharp words,
The gully of greed can never be filled.

Eventually, she stopped leaving her apartment, afraid she would be captured or beaten by government officials. She described her plight as being virtually under house arrest by the time she fled to the United States; it was rumored that she'd be physically detained if she didn't get out.

China's government did not want the world to know that a government-run blood-buying scheme had infected an entire region with a deadly virus. They couldn't get Gao to stop talking about it. Even after she fled to safety in 2007, she kept speaking on it, from an unfamiliar country where she had almost no ties. Each time we met, everything she said, she said with great urgency. And there was one thing Gao repeated every time we spoke: *You need to talk to Wang Shuping. She knows everything.*

———

Wang Shuping was a generation younger and as friendly and sociable as Gao was forceful and argumentative. She created an entirely different life, integrated into her adopted country, lush with friends and family. As I learned more about what had happened in China in the years before I arrived and how this younger doctor discovered the virus sickening patients in the Chinese plasma pool, I made plans. She had never granted interviews about her work or role in exposing the epidemic; apart from one personal essay she published years later, she seemed to put the whole incident behind her.

Finally, on a spring morning in 2018, I drove south from Montana to Utah to meet this woman who might have saved my life through this odd chain of events. I'd heard her name for years, but I didn't know what to expect. I thought we would be revisiting the dark history of events that took place in another country, not opening a window onto one where we both lived now. Within two years of our first meeting, she, too, would be gone.

CHAPTER 1
The Whistleblower

I tell myself that I protected vulnerable and helpless people
and that I have to be strong against evil powers.
—Wang Shuping

Interstate 15 stretches like a flat gray snake in the shadows of the Rocky Mountains, winding along the broad valleys and open fields from Montana through southern Idaho and into Utah's snow-capped Wasatch Range. This is a rapidly changing part of America. In the 2020s, it has weathered a mass building and gentrification boom spurred by a push to the mountains from new wealth, tourists, second-home owners, and tech investment. The Mountain West offers a glimpse of a world of soaring economic inequality. In the spring, the vast valleys are filled with bright yellow canola fields and patches of purple lupine and camas. It is uncluttered, clean, and perhaps as far as one could escape from the cities of China's crowded, industrial Henan province. People come to this part of America now to ski, hike, and kayak; those who live here full-time wrangle with increasing costs for housing—and just about everything else. I can imagine that coming to Utah from the gray urban tangles of Henan or Beijing, two notoriously gritty spots in China, must have been a relief to Wang Shuping. It seemed so, given the amount of time she spent outdoors, hiking the trails in the nearby mountains.

Wang Shuping and I emailed back and forth for a few weeks before we met. Though she hadn't spoken with any journalists at length, she was eager to meet. She said she had read some of what

I had written about the blood scandal and her old colleagues, and enough time and distance had passed that she felt comfortable talking about it.

As I drove the 400-some-mile stretch from my home in Montana down through the valleys, she sent text messages every two hours, giving me directions to her home and checking to see if I was safe on the road. It felt like we already knew each other by the time I pulled up outside her house, a beautiful brick home with a big, well-tended yard and garden. I had been to her hometown back in China; I knew how different this little slice of Americana was from the rural edges of a big Chinese city.

Over the years, I had met many Chinese dissidents, human rights lawyers, and hard-bitten activists—the most outspoken critics of the regime. I'm not sure who I expected Wang Shuping to be, but a small, smiling woman with a quick laugh, who had adopted "Sunshine" as her English name, was probably not it. And yet it fit her perfectly. Dr. Wang's smile was instant; it lit up the room. Her laugh was infectious. She was short, neatly coiffed and dressed, maybe ten years older than me, and we hit it off from the first moment. I stepped out of my car and we hugged hello. It was like visiting an aunt I had just met in person for the first time.

She insisted I stay with her in Salt Lake City, at her large home in the foothills. She welcomed me in, introduced her husband and the pets, and made me feel like a family member. We chatted for a bit about my drive down from Montana, then she told me what she had planned for us for the next few days. She wanted to take a ride to Park City for lunch, then tour around downtown Salt Lake City. We'd see the Mormon temples and tourist sites. There was somewhere else she was eager to take me, but she didn't explain what it was right away. She just made a point of telling me that we needed to stop somewhere, to see a specific place, after our day full of sightseeing.

I was happy to roll along with the tour schedule and let her decide what she wanted to tell me and when. I wanted to hear her story, but I was in no hurry to dive into an interview about what happened back in China. Yet within a few minutes of chatting about my long drive, she asked what she seemed to have been wondering about since I first contacted her.

How to Create a Crisis

"It's been twenty-three years," she said. "Why do you still care about this?" As best as I could, I explained that she might have saved my life in a roundabout way, and she certainly saved many others from exposure to a deadly virus. She nodded her head, now understanding why I had come. As we chatted late into the evening, she stopped abruptly at one point to ask if I was tired. Even though I hadn't thought about it, she noticed that my left hand was trembling—something that happens when I am overly tired. Most people never notice this strange tremor, yet Wang noticed my hand shaking subtly, shortly after we met. She smiled and laughed with ease, but I began to understand how she also noticed tiny details with the careful eye of a trained scientist.

The next morning, we hopped into her hybrid SUV. She asked me to drive because she didn't like to navigate the winding mountain passes. We cruised over the highway for about an hour to reach Park City to the east. Along the way, while traversing a gorgeous winding mountain road, we talked about Chinese food, the landscape, American politics, and, of course, the blood trade in both countries.

Park City is the wealthiest small town in America, a picturesque mountain town filled with tidy, expensive homes, quaint shops, and pricey restaurants. On this Saturday, it was filled with tourists. As we spoke about her fleeing China to the United States, I overheard two women at the next table talking about their housekeepers. The worlds of those two tables were so far apart. I wondered what the women with household staff might think if they knew the petite lady in the white jacket and pants sitting a few feet from them had aggravated the Chinese government so much that she had to run to safety and restart her life in America. That this woman had ended her career and personal life in her home country, a consequence of protecting poor people from a government-managed catastrophe.

Over lunch, I came to understand that Wang had not forgotten the crisis she uncovered, any more than I was able to ignore the plasma industry I rely on for survival. It was clear she remembered all that had happened back in China, and those events shaped the facets of her life. Wang had an optimism about the world that often eluded others who challenged China's power structure and subsequently fled for their lives. Even so, I could tell that it was on her mind all the time. When we finished eating and started the drive back to Salt Lake City, she reminded me again there was something in an otherwise unremarkable strip mall near her house she wanted to show me. We made a plan to go the following day. That night, she told me more of her story.

Wang grew up on the other side of the world from Salt Lake City, outside of Zhoukou, a bustling metropolis that sits at the confluence of three rivers in Henan province. I'd been to Zhoukou a few times while reporting on electronics manufacturing in China. The region had become a cheaper hub for companies like Apple to make their devices, hiring farm kids who accepted lower wages than offered in other, bigger factory towns. That city in the mid-2010s was dirty, industrial, and gray, the rivers choked with waste and tainted by chemical pollution. China changes fast and often unpredictably, but I got the feeling Zhoukou was last on the list of cities slated for improvements. It seemed to be a place forgotten or pushed aside in the rush for prettier, greener versions of development in metropolises, like Beijing and Shanghai.

Wang came of age in the tumultuous years of China's Cultural Revolution, when political upheaval touched every life, especially of those in the countryside. Mao's great uprising destroyed educational systems, smashed cultural foundations, and made "re-education" the rule of the land. Even so, Wang worked her way through the mess and studied science and medicine at university. She was drawn to the sciences and public health, interests of hers from as far back as she could remember.

Early in her career, in 1991, she was assigned to a health department in the city of Zhoukou, hired in an intriguing new role: medical researcher tasked with monitoring the health of donors in the city's first blood plasma extraction center. The plasma bank paid its donors the equivalent of seven to eight U.S. dollars for half a liter of blood, under the banner of a government program that touted unproven health benefits and potential wealth for blood sellers. News spread rapidly among the farmers, who were used to backbreaking labor and little money. This was easy cash—guaranteed pay for something they had plenty of. A few weeks after opening, there were

200 people a day lining up at the plasma bank to donate their blood protein. They crowded the clinic rooms and snaked in lines through the corridors to have their veins tapped for cash. The clinics rushed those plasma donors through the process as if they were livestock, extracting the plasma as quickly as possible to get ever more raw material that could be sold for profit.

At the time, Wang was looking for hepatitis C—a virus that travels in the blood and inflames the liver—and she found it already had infiltrated the plasma pool. She hunted for signs that the emergency had arrived, knowing it was only a matter of time before the human immunodeficiency virus (HIV) showed up in her testing samples. It finally happened in 1995. A man who traveled across the country while selling his plasma tested positive for HIV. He continued to roam and sell his tainted blood, unwittingly passing the virus along as he stopped to earn the money each plasma station paid him. By the time his infection showed up in the system, the local blood plasma trade had been scaled up to such a size and speed that nurses and technicians reused tubing and needles to save money and time. Worse, they shared the machines that separate whole blood into plasma and red blood cells. In their hurried push to pull plasma from blood and get donors through the system quickly, the clinics exposed healthy plasma sellers to blood-borne viruses.

Though the practice of selling blood plasma was as stigmatized in China then as it has been in the rest of the world, the payment lured people in. It felt like an easy way to make more money in a matter of minutes than most people had seen in their lifetimes. But across Henan and nearby parts of central China, government clinics rushing to make a profit had cut corners and infected untold thousands of their patients with a deadly virus. Wang sounded the alarm, initially going through low-level government channels at home, then later notifying health authorities in Beijing. At first, they did nothing.

For months after China's leadership knew of the problem—alerted at several points by Wang Shuping as part of her work monitoring the health of donors—the plasma banks stayed open, spreading the virus unchecked among people who came to sell their blood. AIDS treatment was in its infancy, especially in China, and education was the primary resource in helping people avoid the virus. But there was little education, just a continued frenzy to make money from the blood of poor people. Without explaining to the donors that they had been exposed to HIV, a deadly disease, the government suddenly shut down the entire plasma economy. It was then that Wang understood the drive for money and power superseded the health and lives of China's least-protected people. She continued working on the edges of the health-care system for a few more years, documenting the crisis as the disease began killing those early plasma sellers.

Around the same time, Dr. Gao Yaojie found the virus in a patient hundreds of miles away, making it clear AIDS had arrived. The pair began covertly working together to expose the outbreak and its cover-up. With Wang behind the scenes, feeding facts and data to the older doctor, and Gao out front with her guts and iron will, their efforts threatened and alarmed China's top pillars of power, as well as citizens' faith in their health system.

For her trouble, Wang told me, she was threatened, harassed, physically beaten at her testing lab, and released from her job at the clinic. She was nervous but carried on. She continued to spend her own money to run tests and track the AIDS outbreak, but local government officials made it clear she was courting danger at home. To escape the eye of the storm, she took a research job with a mentor in Beijing. Still, she kept her ties open to Henan and gathered data that she would later feed to Dr. Gao and others, who simultaneously kept up the pressure campaign on the government to address the epidemic.

Eventually, even though she was just in her thirties, exposing the AIDS outbreak killed Wang's career prospects in China. The only way forward, the only safe path, lay in getting out of China. She quietly began applying for jobs in the United States and eventually landed a job in Wisconsin, then later Utah. Along the way, she married a kind Midwesterner named Gary. In Salt Lake City, the couple spent weekends hiking with a group of friends. She worked in liver cancer research at the University of Utah. It was a calm, quiet existence, but what had happened back in her homeland was never far from her mind.

On that sunny Sunday evening in Salt Lake, Wang Shuping and

I hopped back into her SUV and drove fifteen minutes to the nearby strip mall. We were going to a U.S. plasma extraction center, a Bio-Life Plasma clinic, that she drove past each day on her way to work. She was eager to see where Americans lined up to offer their veins for money, comparing the scene to what she had witnessed in China. It was not the same; it was cleaner and much more modern. But she was concerned. In the mall parking lot, a man sat inside his open car, pressing a bandage into the cleave of his elbow as he dragged on a cigarette. The scene put on display his tired aftermath of selling plasma to technicians in white coats behind the door.

As we watched, we debated our approach. We decided to ask questions as though we were donors, hoping they would let us see the extraction room. Wang was eager to look over the machinery and the safety guidelines. I was a reporter there to ask questions and along for the trip, but also a patient seeing how the raw materials that made my medication were extracted from human bodies.

I went to Utah to better understand the crisis back in China, believing that, thanks to her, I'd escaped a virus or worse by smuggling in my blood-borne drug supply. I had spent most of my adult life in China, but I fell into the easy trap of idealizing my home country, the United States. Years of reporting on dark stories in a country that wasn't my own allowed me to believe that America was much better. I wasn't unusual in this regard. It's a trick the mind plays when you live far from home, allowing you to believe home is a better place than where you are. Yet my detective mission with Wang erased some of the fog and opened my eyes to how the United States—though its blood supplies are safe—was deep into another kind of exploitative endeavor that centers on the extraction and sale of human blood parts. Wang led me into the unknown, this time in my own backyard.

We pulled open the glass door of the plasma center and stepped up to the counter, noticing the half dozen bored donors sitting there, and one woman tending to some young kids, all waiting in plastic chairs to be called for their turn. A fresh-faced blond man behind the counter in a white lab coat mistook us for potential donors and described the process in detail, cheerfully, in a way that almost made it seem like fun. He assured us that the needle stick wouldn't hurt and that there was no chance of contamination in the process. The payment outlined on a blackboard near the counter spelled out cash bonuses for first-time donors. The more often someone returned, as frequently as twice a week, the higher the pay per donation. The system was clearly designed to encourage people to give as much plasma as possible, for as long as they could. Wang smiled as he explained the lengthy safety rules, then asked him a single question. She wanted to know which day of the week they closed.

She winced a bit when he told her they didn't.

I couldn't at first figure out why this question was important to her, but then it became clear. The churn—the constant in and out of donors—reminded her of the heady days of the plasma economy in China when people lined up in the hallways and out the door to get their payments for blood. What was happening in this country seemed to her too much like what had happened back in China. An identical viral outbreak is nearly impossible in the United States now. In the 1980s, companies that bought and sold plasma started treating the fluid with heat to kill viruses. It worked. When AIDS ravaged central China, that now essential safety protocol was unknown.

As we drove back to her home, Wang talked about the necessary business of medicine—how plasma is needed to treat diseases like mine. What troubled her was that the rush she had seen back in China seemed to now be playing out in her American neighborhood: the brazen pursuit of profit. She shook her head, telling me it was shocking to her that they stayed open every day, even in Salt Lake City, where the religious influence keeps many businesses closed down on Sundays.

Wang had already watched the rush for blood money turn deadly on the other side of the world. What happened in China all those years ago is not going to happen in the United States. What's happening here is different. It's quieter, less deadly, but perhaps more insidious because of how successfully it's been hidden and allowed to grow.

We've built an entire segment of global medicine upon the certainty that some number of Americans simply can't live on a regular income alone. They need blood money to supplement their wages and make their lives easier. And we don't exactly know if or how this frequent extraction of blood proteins might harm their bodies in the long run.

At that moment, I realized all those years I spent smuggling blood into China, trusting the American-made blood apparatus to spare me from China's "inferior" ethics and regulations, had given me a false sense of security. While the process in the United States is sounder, there is potential damage lurking in the spaces we ignore. We don't know all the possible effects. Leeching blood from the poor and selling it for profit created calamity in China; something equally calamitous could happen here, again.

————

That spring and summer, Wang Shuping and her husband often spoke of the daughter of a family friend, Frances Ya-Chu Cowhig, a playwright in London who was writing a production about the doctor's life and heroism. After all the years of keeping her secrets, Wang was ready to talk about her activism in China. But for someone who had lived through years of government pressure and bullying, I was surprised during our visits when Wang would ask me, entirely without cynicism, whether I thought it would be safe for her to return to China, just to visit. I told her what I'd seen in recent years, how the government had grown harder and less tolerant of criticism. "No," I said, "I don't think it's safe for you." She didn't seem to quite register how bad things had become. It was difficult to explain how the government's power grip on people's lives had tightened so significantly since she left her home country. She never did return to China, giving up her dream to bring her husband, Gary, to Henan and Beijing so he could eat authentic Chinese food.

In the fall of 2019, she and Gary instead traveled to London to see the opening performance of *The King of Hell's Palace*, the play about her work that was produced at the Hampstead Theatre. I spoke with her before she left and she was thrilled to finally be able to see her life and work depicted onstage. But in the weeks leading up to that premiere, the Chinese government pressed its heavy hand against Wang Shuping, twenty-four years after she had left that country. Even though she no longer lived there, she became the focus of a Chinese government pressure campaign.

Back in China, local cops and thugs began threatening Wang's family, the regime stretching out powerful tentacles in a familiar pattern of bullying for political purposes. Two decades on, the Chinese government refused to fully reckon with the deadly crisis it had caused in that one region, and it deployed a pressure campaign across three countries—the United States, England, and China—to keep that crisis cloaked in silence.

Wang refused to be quiet, however. She had held her tongue for too long. She released a statement detailing how her family had been bullied. She reaffirmed her support for the play and her intent to keep speaking out about the Henan AIDS crisis.

> *I am in America now, and am a U.S. citizen. . . . I tell myself that I protected vulnerable and helpless people and that I have to be strong against evil powers. I hope the play helps expose and stop the kinds of corruption and bullying Chinese doctors, health officials, and AIDS activists like Dr. Gao Yaojie, [fellow activist] Wan Yanhai, and myself endured during our efforts to draw attention to the Henan AIDS epidemic of the 1990s.*

Wang returned to Salt Lake City in September of that year. We traded a few messages, making vague plans to meet at some point in the future. I invited her to Montana and said maybe I'd get back to Salt Lake for a long weekend so we could catch up. She was delighted about the success of the play, and she spoke with enthusiasm that maybe the Chinese government would finally have to acknowledge the deaths and suffering it had caused.

Within weeks, she was gone. While hiking with her husband and some friends in the nearby Wasatch Mountains, Wang suffered a sudden heart attack and died. She was just 59 years old. She had spent more than half her life refusing to bow to power, and she had experienced the consequences of it. I would never be able to prove it, but it felt to me as though she had been hounded to death for speaking out against a powerful regime and a secret it wanted buried.

———

Through our conversations, I began to understand that Wang Shuping worried about the state of her adopted country as well. When we met, the United States was deep into the tense years of the fractured, racist politics of the Trump presidency, and she had trouble recognizing the place she had chosen to call home. Even as we spoke about the plasma scandal back in China, she would veer back into concerns about what was happening in contemporary America.

China invented that macabre scheme and gave it a name, the "plasma economy," a driver of their economic engine powered by medicines and research made from people's blood. That country's attempt at it was comparatively short-lived and perhaps more deadly than any similar attempt elsewhere in the world. But if China had come up with the notion to use blood to undergird parts of its economy, private industry in the United States had been building and perfecting that plan all along, calling it nothing so concrete and avoiding too much attention on it. A key difference lies in who controls the system. Profit-making companies and scientific and medical research are built upon the backs of people who struggle financially in this society, just as they were in China. Here, we don't see it so much as a cohesive, deliberate plan.

In the United States, the scale of the plasma economy is hidden from people who live comfortably and don't need to sell their blood for gas or groceries. When I launched into what would become a journey through several of the blood extraction hubs of America, I had no idea how widespread the practice was. It's hidden, too strange or awful to contemplate too deeply for most people. It is woven into our society. In the course of investigating where my medication comes from, I discovered this practice reaches far and deep into our union, pulling in millions of people whose wages for regular jobs aren't sufficient, whose student loan repayments are bankrupting them, or sometimes those who just want to take a nice vacation.

I have listened several times to a recording of my last interview with Wang Shuping. It was a long chat as we sat at her kitchen table. As we talked, she seemed insistent that I find out more about the plasma economy in the United States. She did not trust what she saw going on here, after having lived through the plasma catastrophe in

China. What had happened there could also happen here—maybe not with a deadly viral bomb in our current medical environment, but perhaps through other dangers to Americans, especially the most vulnerable. On that promise, I set out to find the plasma sellers in America and learn why they do it, and at what costs.

CHAPTER 2
The Sellers

People shouldn't have to be struggling for $40
to pay the rent in the first place.
—Darryl Lorenzo Wellington, playwright, novelist, and poet

In late October 2014, a 35-year-old woman and her boyfriend pulled into a generic-looking Florida strip mall in Jacksonville. They walked into a business called DCI Biologicals, where she attempted to sell her blood plasma. The clinic, tucked into the development beside a Dollar Store on the city's west side, was buzzing with patients and lab techs—one tiny cog in the vast industry that pays Americans for their blood plasma. Inside the waiting room, witnesses would later state, other plasma sellers saw the woman swallow several pills while she sat waiting to check in with the staff. When the woman's turn came, she started a loud argument with the center's employees, who told her she wouldn't be allowed to give plasma that day.

It's a thing that happens. Donors are turned away from plasma centers all over the country, every day, for any number of health and safety reasons. Perhaps their protein levels are too low, or they had a recent surgery, or they got a new tattoo. In this case, one of the innumerable items that can go wrong when someone tries to sell plasma did go wrong. The woman was reportedly "deferred" that day and it sent her into a rage.

"I will just kill all of you in the building!" a man in the room later told the Jacksonville police he heard the woman yell as she stormed out of the building and headed to the parking lot. Another witness heard her say she was going to "raise hell," according to the arrest report. The woman returned to her red Honda Accord, started it up, and hit the gas. She accelerated from the parking space straight through the front door of the building. Her car came to a stop forty feet inside the plasma center. A man who had been working at a business next door ran to help, saw the wrecked car, and reached in to grab the keys out of the ignition to stop her from ramming the car further.

The car's impact crushed the plasma center's front counters and some support beams, collapsing most of the roof and injuring a dozen people inside. The woman, Pamela Miller, eventually pleaded "no contest" to aggravated assault, a felony. If she had been allowed to sell her plasma and go home, the day probably would have ended with her having an extra $20 in her pocket. Instead, she was sentenced to thirty months in prison followed by ten years of probation.

When I began investigating the long trail leading back to the origins of my medication, I assumed most plasma was collected from a tiny sliver of the American population—maybe a few hundred thousand people a year—selling their blood parts to earn a little extra money. As I dug in, though, I found that it is, in fact, millions of people each year pushed to the clinics by small events, like needing gas money, groceries, vacations. Once in a while, as in the case of Pamela Miller, the situation escalates too far.

I heard about Pamela Miller's car crash years after the incident from writer Darryl Lorenzo Wellington. Back in 2014, Wellington wrote a piece for the *Atlantic* magazine about his experiences as a plasma seller. His writing gave me a first clue that the medication I'd been relying on for years, made with U.S. blood plasma, might have dark origin stories. To be honest, I had been hiding from the truth of the matter, and reading Wellington's reporting shook me out of a peaceful delusion about why the United States produces so much blood plasma. I'm not sure how I ever believed the idea that Americans were more altruistically giving of their essential parts than people in other countries, more willing to donate their plasma to feed the world's demands. So much of the world's blood plasma comes from the United States, but that's not because we are an especially altruistic society.

Around the world, most developed nations prohibit paying people to give blood or plasma. Yet in the United States, where financial struggles have been on the rise for generations, as wages and benefits have failed to keep up since the punishing economic politics of Ronald Reagan in the 1980s, blood plasma has grown into a substantial American export. Generations of people who struggle economically have made selling plasma a normal, commonplace practice. In 2021, American blood products accounted for more than $24 billion in worldwide sales and were 2.69 percent of the United States' total exports. That's a higher percentage than soybeans and several other crops that are sold overseas. A substantial portion of the blood plasma used all around the world comes from the veins of people in the United States.

In other words, we sell more blood products to other countries than we do some of the world's most common farm goods. This bizarre state of affairs has created a catchphrase among economists and others when discussing the global blood trade: they call the United States the "OPEC of plasma." In other words, so much of the world's bought-and-sold blood parts originate in the United States that it's comparable to a global oil cartel. The three plasma extraction companies that own and operate the greatest numbers of paid plasma centers in the U.S. are owned by biomedical giants in Spain and Australia, with their products sold around the world, making it a truly globalized economic endeavor.

In practical terms, this means that while a patient in Switzerland with my identical illness might frown on the idea of people selling their plasma, she is likely getting a medication made from the blood of Americans who have, essentially, sold their body parts.

It is easy to dismiss this as an American problem, but it's a problem that fuels the world. Plasma from the United States travels the globe and flows into global medicines. The cutthroat capitalism that powers the U.S. blood plasma economy shifts the burden of thinking about paid plasma away from citizens of countries with robust social safety nets that don't need to be backfilled by unsavory things like selling their blood.

When I spoke with Darryl Wellington in 2021, he had just been named poet laureate of Santa Fe, New Mexico, and was busy juggling a full a schedule of writing and speaking events. His plasma-selling days are long past, but his memories of what he saw and experienced in those centers remained fresh. We spoke by phone, as I had with so many people for this undertaking. I was reporting in the midst of a pandemic that might have killed me, before vaccines became available and made the possibility of contracting COVID-19 slightly less terrifying.

A Different Type of Tired

Darryl Wellington was broke back in the early 2010s, and he needed some extra money to supplement his income as a freelance writer and substitute teacher. Left with few choices for earning that extra for rent and to pay bills, he sold his plasma half a dozen times. In doing so, he stepped into the weird world of clinical plasma harvesting, of plasma sellers putting their health on the line for payments delivered to them on prepaid debit cards that often charge fees when used. In Wellington's case, that first turn with the plasma extractor wiped him out for a day, exhausted by the loss of protein and fluid. That's because the exhaustion from losing plasma can feel like it drains the body almost to the bones. He described it as "a different type of tired. It feels like there's something foreign in your body."

Wellington donated plasma a few more times because he needed to, but he couldn't fathom becoming one of those seasoned regulars. The procedure was too hard on his body. He did get to know other donors and the people who worked in the plasma center, however, and he wrote about them in that *Atlantic* article, a story so stark and so revealing that, in the months after, he got dozens of calls and emails from others who had sold their plasma to make ends meet. Many of them, he recounted, were strangely defensive about the practice and the companies that engaged in the extraction. Many had darker stories than his. One of the people who contacted him was Pamela Miller's attorney. Could the exploitative nature of selling plasma drive someone to lash out or react in a strange physical manner, or go to extreme ends, like crashing their car into a building? The attorney wanted to know.

Wellington laughed when he remembered the exchange, as if it was so ridiculous that all you can do is laugh. It isn't the *act* of selling plasma that could make someone do something desperate; it's the socioeconomic conditions that lead someone to sell plasma that could do that. But dire poverty isn't even the root problem in all of this; it's more the difficult balance of trying to work and earn a decent living. In talking with more than 100 plasma sellers over the course of two years, I found that most people are simply looking for extra income. It's not a primary means of making a living. These are people who work full-time, or are university students, or folks paying off debts of one sort or another.

That's exactly how the system is designed. Selling plasma does not pay enough to live on; it pays just enough to fill the gas tank or the refrigerator. The practice targets the working class and people we like to call the "working poor"—often those who earn enough to live in permanent housing and own cars, but who are on the edge of having too little money to make everything flow just right. "We have the right kind of people in poverty you can play with," Wellington told me. "You're surrounded by wealth, and you're not really poor. You make a modest income in a wealthy country but because of the prices that people charge you, you're poor."

That is, I think, a good description of America's working classes and poor. A study released in 2022 by the antipoverty organization Oxfam America showed that nearly one-third of American workers earn less than $31,000 per year, or $15 per hour when working 40 hours a week. The number of people in that bracket are disproportionally women and people of color. The study found that 47 percent of Black workers and 46 percent of Hispanic workers made under $15 an hour, far more workers than the 26 percent of white employees who earned less than $15 hourly. Forty percent of women earned less than $15 an hour, compared with 25 percent of men. An entire class of Americans struggles to get by—absent social safety nets, universal health care, strong labor union protections, and decent minimum wages that keep pace with the cost of living in this country.

That low wage—$15 an hour—is almost exactly what I made as a local newspaper reporter twenty years earlier, and it was a tight budget to live on as a single person, even back then. Somewhere around 52 million people pay rent and buy groceries and gas on $31,000 a year, which brings into focus why they might need the extra money from selling plasma to pay off a debt, to go to the movies, or to take a vacation. Earlier federal antipoverty programs, gutted beyond usefulness by generations of trickle-down economics that began with Reagan's presidency in the 1980s, have left the non-rich with little other choice but to take on second and third jobs to make ends meet. Years of economic studies have shown that tax cuts for the wealthy have been linked to stagnant wage growth for the rest of us; the result has been a steadily higher cost of living and a subsequent hollowing out of the middle class. For many, that's where selling plasma comes in. In a lot of cases, it is easier, quicker, and far less exhausting than getting a second or third minimum-wage or low-paying job. It's a hassle, but what isn't?

Something else Darryl Wellington said stuck with me as I began to plan out a journey through the maze of cities and towns filled with people who are just broke enough to sell their body: "People shouldn't have to be struggling for $40 to pay the rent in the first place."

It makes perfect sense that an entire industry preying upon the cells extracted from people's bodies has emerged in a landscape where the economics of life work against them and there aren't many other options. The plasma business is just a symptom of something bigger; it's almost a natural outgrowth of what has gone wrong in the American economic landscape in the past few decades. As the rich have gotten richer, the not-rich have been pushed further into strange, sometimes desperate, sidelines.

———

When I heard the story of Pamela Miller's car crash into the Florida plasma extraction clinic, I had been using a medication made from the parts of other people's blood for twenty years. Per my rough calculations, by that time I'd had somewhere around 200 infusions, usually once every six weeks, year after year. Sometimes the illness faded into remission, and I went months without needing a treatment, but it's always lurking in the background. The sheer volume of other people's cells that have entered my bloodstream is overwhelming to think about. It's hard not to see myself as a living vampire, enabled by modern medicine and the failures of capitalism. Each time

I go to the clinic for an infusion, the origins of those cells that keep my body functioning pushes a fluttering little rise of anxiety up from my stomach and into my chest. I don't know that I'd have the same feeling if it were an injection of chemicals made in a lab. Somehow, knowing the genesis of those cells is the lifeblood of other people's bodies adds to the anxiety.

Vampire Scars

The backs of both my hands are a spiderweb of tiny white and pink scars, a road map showing where dozens of nurses in several cities on both sides of the Pacific have punctured the thin skin with a needle, leaving inside the vein a tiny plastic tube that allows medication to flow directly into my bloodstream. Those scars have been expensive. In a typical year, the medicine I use annually adds up to more than $100,000, most of which is paid for by my health insurance. The years are never all that typical, and it's always a bit more or a bit less, but that's the general number. The treatment is called intravenous human immunoglobulin (IVIG, in medical shorthand).

In all these years of reading the carefully folded reams of package inserts and dense scientific papers on the subject, I've never found an easy, plain explanation of how or why it works so effectively on my rare disease. A few doctors I've asked have responded with something along the lines of "We don't really know why it works, but it does."

Lest anyone believe it is faked or imagined, know that it is real. The nerve damage is measurable. What is not known is exactly why placing other people's immune cells inside my own body helps.

There are a few tangible things I do know: Each dose takes five mind-numbingly dull hours to drip into my hand. Each batch might contain cells from thousands of different people. And each session at the infusion center costs my insurance company more than $10,000. The cost varies, often by month, sometimes doubling when I've done nothing more than change insurance companies. Overnight, the price can go up or down. The reasons for the drug price fluctuations are never clearly explained, but speculation points to shortages here and company consolidations there. In 2021, one drug company started paying my health insurance deductible, which came to thousands of dollars a year, in exchange for access to my medical records. I still don't know exactly why they did it, but giving up my privacy seemed an easy way to eliminate some of my medical bills.

There are some upsides to getting the immune system particles of other people. I rarely get colds or the flu—perhaps an offshoot of something called "passive immunity." Filling my veins with other people's immune cells could protect me from the illnesses those people have already had and have built up antibodies against. But when I *do* get sick, it can ignite my temperamental immune system and cause it to attack me, sending my limbs into panicky numbness, along with whatever sniffles and cough an ordinary virus might bring. Though multiple studies have shown no evidence that IVIG works to protect a recipient against COVID-19, each infusion I had in the wake of the pandemic that began in 2019 made me feel a tiny bit of relief, a sense that maybe I'm protected by virtue of others. That weird, perhaps even false, sense of communal protection, pushed into my veins by force with an electric pump, did help psychologically in the absence of a cohesive government response to that deadly threat.

IVIG is the most common product made from America's giant plasma pool. In the United States are several brands—sold under similar names, like Gamunex-C, Gammagard, and Gammaplex—and each uses a slightly different proprietary mix to do roughly the same thing. Some brands make me less sick in the days after an infusion than others, but they all do the job.

The flush of panic I feel at the start of an infusion is not my own lingering fear of needles—a fear I learned to cope with long ago. It's knowing that my medication is built on the backs of quiet, hidden economic desperation. Those bags full of cloudy yellow liquid have been squeezed out of the class of our society that mostly doesn't have big savings accounts, or well-off parents who can help with rent or mortgage, or jobs that pay well enough to not need the little extra cash that selling plasma provides.

It's soothing in our minds to believe that people who give plasma do so for purely altruistic reasons—the same way we've been encouraged to donate blood regularly and give more when disaster strikes. But by now, I know better. My survival, or at least my ability to function without serious physical disability, is dependent on the plasma from many of America's economically marginalized, as well as our refusal to do better by them. The *vampire* part of this situation is funny, to a degree, but the economics of blood plasma are not. That is, I physically depend on a certain number of people desperate enough to sell off a part of themselves. All these weirdly named medicines work like magic on my broken immune system—incredibly expensive magic made from the exploitation of people fallen on hard times.

There's no small amount of guilt in knowing that your continued health and ability to function relies on the financial hardships of others, potentially millions of people each year who live just on the edge and on the wrong side of the American economic balance. Because the industry is shrouded in secrecy and the legions of people who sell their plasma are often stigmatized and dismissed as "the poor," unworthy of attention, their true numbers are difficult to pin down. There are a lot of clues, however, that enable a pretty well-educated guess that the total is much higher than most people know.

I began my investigation by understanding a few basics: Plasma centers receive more than 50 million donations per year, and, at the absolute maximum, donors are allowed to contribute 104 times each year, but according to the Plasma Protein Therapeutics Association, only 14 percent of donors give more than fifty times per year. The medicine that sustains me has to be drawn from a deep, overlooked pool of millions of Americans often moving in and out of periods of economic precarity. The system depends on this. Blood plasma is frequently pulled from people at their lowest points, when struggling through college, scraping by on minimum wage, doing without their own health insurance.

"Selling a Piece of My Body Was the Only Way to Make Rent"

I knew the plasma industry I managed to avoid in China was dirty. For a time, it lured the country's poorest with promises of wealth, then left them ill, broken, and frequently dead. When I moved back to the United States in 2016, I expected our version of the industry to be a niche enterprise, a last resort that helped people deal with extreme poverty. The initial numbers I came across when trying to figure out this puzzle were a guess—that perhaps several hundred thousand Americans sell their plasma each year. I was way off the mark.

The true numbers, in all likelihood, run into many millions of people every year. This is not a niche population; it is a large and growing legion of blood sellers who power the American plasma economy and, in turn, the world's plasma economy. The biggest players in the industry are headquartered outside the United States. The plasma sellers are not usually seen or heard; perhaps it's a story too dark for most of us to take on. If I didn't depend on that economy myself, I don't know that I ever would have been interested in finding out how many people do it or why. Plasma sellers often speak about it in whispers, knowing full well how it's been stigmatized in our society; I had chosen to believe it's a small side hustle for a few people on the margins who rely on the system for money.

While trying to get a grasp on the scale of the plasma extraction business, on a whim I posted a survey on Twitter, asking people if they had ever sold plasma. I expected a few people would chime in. More than 600 people responded. While, yes, I know, it's entirely unscientific to query a social media audience, the numbers still caught me by surprise. Almost 20 percent of the people who responded said they had sold plasma at least once in their lives. This was even more remarkable in a social media space dominated by white-collar professionals.

The responses flooded in from a range of people, from journalists, to adjunct professors, to people who did it in college and stopped but remembered it well. I asked those surveyed to get in touch to talk about their experiences, and about fifty wrote to me with more details about selling plasma. Some of their answers were sad, some were funny, some expressed interest in maybe, perhaps, supplying a recipient in need out there somewhere, but every single person said their decision to sell their blood plasma came down to cold, hard cash. Helping people was a side benefit, always.

One man used the payments to buy a gift for his wife. Another told me a little story about how a relative sold his plasma in secret for years to pay for the services of sex workers, which eventually led to a minor family scandal and a marriage separation. I was beginning to learn that the hidden world of blood money fuels all sorts of lives, and it is not exclusive to the worst-off people in this country, not by a long shot. It's a bridge when regular income isn't enough, which is more common than we allow ourselves to imagine.

Two-thirds of the people I heard from in that survey had sold plasma more than ten times, while the rest were a mix. As to whether the practice paid fairly, the response was split relatively evenly. Many who got in touch felt the practice should pay more to account for their time and the hassle involved. Most were not worried about the potential impact on their health. Still, several revealed some anxiety in regard to whether they had been told the complete truth about the physical toll of giving up plasma for the sellers.

What struck me, too, was the eagerness with which people wanted to talk about selling plasma after being given an invitation to do so. I was surprised by how forthcoming people were, but I got the impression that nobody had asked them in detail about it before. Throughout my research, I interviewed more than 100 plasma donors all over the country. Many didn't want me to use their real names in this book, but apart from that, they were happy to talk.

Some of the responses I received spoke directly to the broken economic conditions of Americans' lives, including the often untenable costs of health care and higher education. Some said they used plasma money to pay down debt piled up from medical bills; others used it for rent and food in college or put it toward their monthly student loan payments. I chatted with more than forty plasma sellers online. All of them said they would or did stop the practice once their debts were paid, once they found a better job, once they were able to dig out of whatever financial hole they'd fallen into. Some couldn't get by without it—the blood money had been integrated into their household budget, contributing to essentials like rent, food, and transportation.

I have heard from public-school teachers, staff journalists, writers, professors, and so many people working in precarious professions or the gig economy who sell their blood plasma. Whereas a job once meant, for many, stable health care and certain other protections, plasma has become the safety net for an awful lot of people, stepping in to cover the gaps created through decades of economic policy shaped in favor of corporations and the wealthy among us. I read through their responses, as varied and interesting as the people themselves. "There were a few years where 'donating' was basically the closest thing I had to health care. I didn't have insurance, and the biannual health check to make sure I wasn't going to die of not enough plasma was the best I got for a while," one woman wrote.

Others spoke about the wealth divide they witnessed in the plasma centers. These places draw in specific segments of our society, from those fallen on temporary hard times to the regulars who depend on it for income. Plasma centers attract the parts of America routinely ignored in media portrayals of the working class. You're much more likely to find America's true working class inside a plasma extraction room than the ubiquitous Rust Belt diners that have become so familiar in our media-generated national consciousness.

"I donated plasma regularly after I lost my job, due to the 2008 recession. I wouldn't have survived without the fast cash of plasma donation. Looking back on it now, I'm pretty horrified that selling a piece of my body was the only way to pay my rent," one plasma seller wrote.

Many plasma sellers say the compensation was never quite enough to make up for time lost and needle sticks, so they gave it up as soon as they were financially able to quit. It helped, but it was barely enough. Those who keep returning to the extraction centers do not love the process, it's a grind and a bore, but they do feel like they need the money. It's a sure payday, until a tech nicks their vein or they faint from dehydration and are banned from donating for a few weeks, losing hundreds of dollars they counted on.

One plasma donor wrote: "I feel that the act of selling plasma— the driving to and from, the giving, the making sure I'd eaten enough protein but not too much fat that day, the excessive shivering, and so on—never quite balanced out with how much I made. Sure, it doesn't hurt, and I'd just sit there reading a book, but it seemed like a lot to just walk away with $20, especially when that $20 was never enough to get me out of the situation of needing to sell plasma for money in the first place."

And though the process is billed as safe and harmless, it is not always innocuous. "They told me to stop. It felt like I had balsa wood in my veins in the donation sites," noted another seller. "Was a good supplement to my student job, was able to stay in school. I got an extra 160 bucks a week for about 5 hours of my time . . . was definitely worth it for me." That same seller also participated in medical trials and rode his bike to and from the sessions. It was a plan that didn't always work out, given the wooziness that sometimes resulted.

Most people, like that donor, saw the whole endeavor with some humor. It's bizarre to sell your blood, everyone knows, and they have to laugh about it sometimes. And then there are the scars, the deep craters I've seen on the arms of countless donors and heard them talk about, with some concern for the stigma it might carry. Though they look nothing like the marks of intravenous drug users, most people don't know the difference. The deep craters left by extended periods of selling plasma are unmistakable. Once you know how they look, you can always spot them. As one donor described, "Sold a lot of plasma 20ish years ago. Got scars on both arms. You gotta love the looks you get at the doctor's office when you have what looks a lot like track marks. Ended up getting the worst one covered with a tattoo."

Some 20 Million Americans a Year

It became clear to me early in this journey that there are a whole lot more people selling their plasma in America than most of us know. I got a sense early on that my guess of hundreds of thousands of people a year was too low. But I still wanted a more tangible number, at least an estimate of the total who do it each year. I spoke at length with Luke Shaefer, director of the Poverty Solutions initiative at the University of Michigan. He and his colleagues have spent years studying poverty in America, turning some of that seminal research into the book *$2.00 a Day: Living on Almost Nothing in America*, coauthored with Kathryn Edin. In their book, investigating the lives of the broke in the United States, Shaefer and Edin reached into the underbelly of paid plasma extraction.

It's an economic endeavor that relies on a myth that most people are selling their plasma as a way to help people like me, not primarily for the money they get by doing it. The opposite is true, it appears. The lack of strict regulation means an accompanying void of hard data about who and how many people sell their plasma. But there are ways to get to a pretty good estimate, Shaefer explained. Starting from bare-bones data, the plasma industry collected a record

53.5 million plasma donations in 2019. Based on the number of raw plasma units sold in one year, Shaefer told me, you can make a pretty good guess that 20 million people or more—nearly 8 percent of the U.S. population of people 18 years or older—might be selling their blood plasma in any given year. It's a back-of-the-envelope calculation, but it tracks with the available data on how much plasma churns through the whirring machines of the blood industry.

Most people who sell their blood plasma are not regular donors, but they'll do it once or twice in a pinch. It's much harder to get a read on the number of people who participate at the maximum level, with twice-weekly trips to the plasma center to earn the most money possible. Anecdotal evidence suggests that it isn't the majority of donors who get hooked into the system at the maximum number of visits a year. Instead, it's likely a mix of newcomers, part-timers, and people who do it long-term as often as possible. This tracks with the people I have spoken with, both online and in person, outside plasma extraction centers around the country. Some do go back for years on end, as often as possible, but it seems like more go a few times, irregularly, and stop as soon as they can. I never heard from anyone who said they missed the practice once they were able to give it up. Among those I talked with, they were all glad to be able to stop when they could.

The estimated number of plasma donors is so high that it is shocking, but also not entirely surprising. In the months since I've started talking with plasma donors and working on this project, nearly everyone I've spoken with is only one or two degrees of separation away from someone else who has sold their plasma for one reason or another. They include the daughters and brothers of friends who are making the cash to pay rent and bills; writers and artists, paid poorly for their work but unwilling to abandon it. College kids looking for a little extra money to have some fun, or just to buy books. The divide is clear among people in my own life, based on who's financially comfortable and who has struggled. Sometimes they'll wait until I've finished explaining the practice to them and then they'll pipe in with "Oh yeah, I did that a few times to make some money."

———

Knowing all this, I began my journey into the world of paid plasma with maps of the United States. I plotted out the precise locations of paid plasma extraction centers across the country—little clusters that spring up and remain in areas where economic inequality, and along with it racial inequality—are often most pronounced. The industry has blown up in dozens of states as our economic gaps have widened. There were fewer than 300 paying plasma centers in 2005 compared with more than 1,000 by 2021. In many parts of this country, the strip-mall plasma extraction center has become as much of a community institution as a Dollar Store or a Walmart.

Next, I needed to find out how many people were paid just enough to draw them in the doors to make something I depend upon, something that's incredibly expensive. The question that was always in the back of my mind: Why can't we come up with a system that's fairer to everyone involved? Luke Shaefer and his colleagues have traced how the rise in plasma extraction has followed the path of socioeconomic discord across the country and found that, in many places, plasma extraction centers emerged in the fault lines.

In the Rust Belt, across the South, along the U.S.-Mexico border, the practice of paying people for their blood plasma thrives in communities where substantial portions of the population live below the federal poverty line. They are communities that tend to be more urban than rural, home to higher-than-average numbers of Black and Hispanic residents, along with more people with lower rates of educational attainment. In short, cities and towns with many people living in tough financial conditions.

As in simple blood donation, plasma donation discriminates against an entire segment of the population. Even though heat processing kills the virus that causes AIDS and is standard today, the ghost of the AIDS epidemic led regulators to bar men who have sex with men from donating plasma unless they've been celibate for three months or longer. Like many practices in the American medical industry, the rule doesn't make much sense based on current science.

The plasma industry did not create the canyons of inequality; they were carved deep by existing streams of racism, classism, and regionalism. But the system does methodically exploit these ravines, geotargeting those most likely to suffer through some of the discomfort and potential fatigue in exchange for relatively easy money. The Mountain West, where I live, is a whiter area than other places and has relatively few clusters of paid plasma extraction centers. That's likely because there are simply fewer people here, even though income inequity is rising.

But across the rest of the country, in the way that pawnshops have been a sign of a community on the ropes, the vampire-like presence of the plasma industry can tell you a lot about a city or town. The red dots on my map connect a pattern of spidery lines and arteries that trace the connections of communities where industries have been hollowed out, where the cost of housing has been rising, or where the border serves to separate American wealth from Mexico's much lower wages.

Where you live matters in this country, for so many reasons. The economic imbalance of it all can be seen by the presence of plasma centers that pay people to extract their blood and spin out the plasma.

I started with my map, scanning the country across regions and states, and I planned to go looking for people who feed the giant pool. I wanted to see what it says about us, as a society, and the ways in which we expect Americans to devise new and increasingly cruel ways to get by. What I found were stories spanning the country, talking with dozens of people who depend on the income. I have no issue with people selling their plasma; I depend on it. The part I find abhorrent is a hardened divide I uncovered in the process of researching this book. Even as millions of people feel financially forced to sell their cells, so many others have never even heard of the practice.

I began this strange journey at a plasma extraction center in Missoula, the closest one to where I lived. Sandwiched between two busy streets, behind a Target, one of Montana's tiny handful of paid-plasma extraction clinics buzzed with traffic from the time the doors opened. A local newspaper story from 2006, before the industry became more secretive, told me the stand-alone brick-and-mortar center is nearly 15,000 square feet and the largest plasma extraction center in Montana. This was when I noticed how the plasma industry made a push through soft features in local newspapers to get more donors during the pre–social media era.

Missoula, the river city where I partly grew up when it was still a gritty, weird timber mill town, is rapidly gentrifying, with housing prices climbing far out of reach for the working people who earn local wages. It's becoming a popular spot for remote workers and second-home owners. The University of Montana and its thousands of students also supply the center with a steady stream of plasma sellers on any given day.

From Dallas, Texas, to Spokane, Washington, to Joplin, Missouri, community newspapers published tales of making easy money by selling plasma, even pitching the practice as a break for over-whelmed parents to sit quietly for an hour while their children wear themselves out in a supervised playroom. The stories explained the process, the altruistic reasons for donating, and the uses of human plasma, but there was rarely discussion of the financial problems that bring many people in to be hooked up to a centrifuge for an hour. Today, these plasma centers rarely let reporters in their doors to see the inner workings. The medical privacy of the donors is a legitimate concern, but a lack of transparency conceals this part of the American economy, one that many people might find intolerable if they knew the gritty details. I asked for and was denied access early on, a rejection that fanned my fascination and my many-months-long investigation.

On this day, I would try to sell plasma, or at least see how far I could get in the process. As a recipient of human blood products, I have been told at several points in my life that I'm banned from donating blood or plasma. It's a safety practice to avoid blood-borne infections, but my own physical health might bar me from selling plasma anyway.

Inside the Missoula center, the fake wood paneling and a dull magazine selection on the counter left the impression this could be any random medical clinic, maybe even the office of an optometrist or dentist. A pleasant brown-haired woman behind the counter greeted me when I walked in, then directed me to a computer kiosk to start answering an intake questionnaire, which would determine whether I qualified. The start of the process is something between applying for a job and an actual medical appointment—waiting in line, filling out computer forms, trying not to stare too much at the others who are waiting. But I didn't get past the first screening questionnaire, so I barely got a peek at how the place operates. It was busy, though; I could see that.

While regular donors logged in and updated their medical information, answering questions about whether they had any new tattoos or recent brushes with needles or new drugs, I halted on the second page of the intake form. Questions 12 through 18 asked if I'd had a blood transfusion or if I had come in contact with anyone else's blood in the past twelve months. In my life, the answer to that question is arguably always yes. Every six weeks, right around the corner from this building in a different clinic, my own blood is infused with cells from other people's plasma. The state of my health might disqualify me anyway, but I'm not making it past the initial form.

I asked the woman at the desk if receiving blood products disqualified me; she nodded yes and I walked out. That's as far as I've ever gotten in trying to experience the sensation of having my plasma extracted. Instead, I know only what it feels like to be the consumer, a vampire aided by machines and hundreds of feet of plastic IV tubing.

———

China may have given a name to the concept of the plasma economy, but the United States ramped it up into a massive industry, wove it into the fabric of this country, and made it prosper. But in the United States, the business isn't confined to one state or a poorer city here or there; it's spread across hundreds of communities, wherever economic conditions have become tough enough to drive people to sell pieces of themselves.

CHAPTER 3
Mormon Country, U.S.A.

I don't even really think
about who gets it.
—Rett Nelson, journalist and plasma seller

When I started off studying the map of plasma extraction centers in bright red and blue dots and clusters around the country, a grouping in Idaho caught my attention partly because it's right next door to where I live in western Montana. I was also intrigued because the Mountain West is not a plasma selling hot spot; there simply aren't that many people living in this part of the United States. Though the Mountain West looms large in the collective American imagination, for me it has always just been home—a remote, misunderstood, and often fetishized place. Idaho is often maligned as a land of racists and far-right politics, but it is, like most places, complicated and diverse. Outside the Mountain West, people often have a skewed perception of Idaho as just a magnet for white nationalism, thanks to the enclaves that have thrived there and threatened parts of the state and country over the years. But I wasn't looking for any of that. I wanted to know what leads people in Idaho to sell their blood plasma. What I found was a complex, very Idaho answer.

The reason seems to lie partly in the service-oriented goals of the Church of Jesus Christ of Latter-day Saints (LDS), which surprised me. This mountain state has many more plasma extraction centers than I would have guessed. And while the region overall is not a major draw for plasma extraction, something interesting is afoot in

Idaho. I didn't expect that my search for the plasma sellers of America would lead me into the heart of Mormon country.

But I should know by now that this part of the United States—the lesser traveled sweep from the edge of southwestern Montana down into Idaho and Utah—is full of the unexpected. Nothing should surprise me, since I grew up nearby and know that things are not always as they're portrayed. As I embarked on a road trip to a remote college town that's almost entirely Mormon, a small city with a larger number of people who sell their plasma than normal, I passed through pieces of my own family's complicated history.

———

As I drove along the highway through this rugged country, past sprawling cattle ranches and the snowy peaks of the Pioneer Range of Montana and the towering Sawtooth Range in Idaho, I thought about my grandmother. She was born in these parts at the turn of the twentieth century in a little mining town called Gilmore, Idaho, near the Montana border. Her parents were on the run then, fleeing the aftermath of a murder in Utah—the details of which I've never been able to quite pin down. Her mother, the youngest child of a large Mormon pioneer family, had been married as a teenager to a man named Smith in Park City, Utah, until she took up with my great-grandfather, a tall, handsome German immigrant who came to the West to work in the silver mines. There was a local crime committed and, in its wake, my great-grandparents fled to southern Idaho, where he could get work in the mines there. They cut their ties with her Mormon family, creating a distance so great, my grandmother never spoke of it.

This might seem wild and weird, but violent crime is not an uncommon part of the origin stories for settler families with deep roots in the Mountain West. The details are often murky and tough to fact-check. What I know is that when my great-grandfather was injured in a mining accident in Gilmore, the growing family picked up stakes and moved again. This time, they brought my grandmother and her siblings to Butte, Montana, just as the 1918 flu pandemic was ripping through the city and its booming population of young miners and their families.

I have thought about my grandmother often when I've met peo-ple selling their plasma to get through life. She grew up so poor that she had to quit high school to work and earn money by help-ing take care of the family of a wealthy doctor in Butte. Eventually, she was able to return to school and become a nurse, a job at which she thrived. She often told me stories of medical mysteries, of good doctors saving patients who had suffered health disasters. But her birthplace is now a ghost town. The most interesting thing to happen there in recent years was when someone shot at four police officers passing through, from what appeared to be an abandoned building, in 2009. Butte, Montana, where she finally settled, has shrunk to a much smaller version of itself as the Mountain West has grown ever more gentrified, its storied mining history giving way to film sets and the "recreation economy."

That recreation economy is an optimistic way of describing tourism-fueled service-industry jobs that don't pay enough to afford soaring housing prices—or much of anything else. My grandmother, who was able to climb out of poverty with steady, hard work and build a middle-class life in the twentieth century, when that was much more possible, died before selling blood would become a com-mon means of survival for a lot of Americans. I know she would have had some unfavorable opinions about it.

All these thoughts rolled through my mind as I followed the gentle curves of I-15 heading southward, passing through the worn, rowdy cowboy towns of southwestern Montana, crossing into Idaho, where the texture of the road changes ever so slightly. Since it was winter, the bad road made it obvious the snowplows didn't pass by here quite so often. The last time I took this drive, I was on my way to meet Wang Shuping in Salt Lake City. As I traveled this time, it had been nearly two years since Dr. Wang died of a sudden heart at-tack on a hiking trail—two years in which the COVID-19 pandemic changed the world, taking the lives of more than 800,000 Americans by the time I hit the road. It seems so bizarre that a woman who staked her life on defending the victims of a different pandemic, on the other side of the world, didn't live long enough to see this one ravage the country where she had chosen to live.

Going deeper south into true Mormon country, I remembered how one thing that had bemused Dr. Wang about living in Utah was the gentle, persistent drumbeat of attempts to convert her to the Church of Jesus Christ of Latter-day Saints. The last time we dined together in Salt Lake City, she giggled about their insistent, gentle nudging, making me consider how people trying to sway her to a new religion had no idea they were dealing with a woman who had shaken the foundations of power in China. The larger cultural and societal norms of Mormonism—attitudes of community and social sharing—worked well for a woman who had grown up believing in the power of collective action during Mao's time. But she had no interest in joining any organized religion, and Mormonism seemed about as far-fetched to her as any other religious belief.

This rugged, mountainous part of the country—along the spine of the Northern Rockies extending through Idaho, western Montana, and into Utah—looks like the imagination's conception of the American West. What's often forgotten is how this part of America was shaped in part by followers of the Mormon Church. The church remains strong to this day, with its persistent, flawed, and frankly often racist Western mythology of wide-open spaces, white men in cowboy hats, and fierce independence. Its influence has, in recent years, led to a massive influx of people and wealth, largely fed by newly remote workers seeking a piece of the Western dream. Their push inward has pushed others out, forcing an even greater chasm between the haves and have-nots of the West.

As housing and other costs continue to grow, working-class residents of the region have been pushed into finding different means to get by. The plasma business apparently has taken notice. For generations, one of the hallmarks of the Mountain West was its relatively low rate of economic inequality compared with the rest of the United States. That, along with the region's low population density, ensured this would not be an ideal place for the plasma extraction industry to take root. But that's all changing fast.

In places like Salt Lake City, Utah, and Boise, Idaho, residents routinely make trips to the local plasma center to offer up a vein for cash. In Rexburg, Idaho, where I headed on that winter morning, selling blood plasma is so taken for granted that it carries a fainter stigma of poverty than I have seen in other parts of the country. There doesn't seem to be much thinking about it beyond pure pragmatism in Rexburg; you sell your blood plasma to pay for what you need and it comes with the benefit of helping someone down the road, someone you'll probably never meet.

There's Something About Rexburg

Like just about any other small town in America, people here generally seem leery of outsiders who ask lots of questions, but not so much when it comes to the plasma question. One of the first people I talked with about Rexburg was Rett Nelson, who works as a journalist in Idaho Falls, a larger city about half an hour away. He went to college in Rexburg and has rooted himself in the town to report on the community and the plasma industry there. He tells me he sold his plasma for years. It's a practice he took up to make money as a college student more than a decade ago, and it has filled some financial gaps for him since then. These days, he commutes thirty miles each way to work, and the money from selling plasma every so often—he tries to hold off until he gets good coupons—offsets the cost of his gas. Nelson is friendly, but in the blunt and direct way of many Westerners. He was the first person I spoke with who didn't soft-pedal his reasons for going back to the plasma center.

Nelson has a scar inside the crook of his elbow, a divot dug deep from the many times a wide needle and catheter have pierced the spot, but it does not concern him. It is, he said, above all about the money. This is strikingly different; most try to soften it a bit, mentioning the part about giving back to society while acknowledging the incentive of money. That's fair, given the financial straits that make it difficult for people to donate money or time to charitable causes. But when I chatted with Nelson, he didn't pretend to care all that much. "I don't even really think about who gets it," he told me.

I felt compelled to tell him I'm one of those people who reaps the benefit of his donation. He didn't seem all that impressed, but then, why would I expect him to be? This sense of detachment is more common than is let on by most plasma donors I've spoken to, but the dynamic of the conversation often changes when I tell them I use a medication that might have been made from their cells. They seem glad, for the most part, to know that the fluid extracted from their body is being used to help someone.

Sometimes the plasma sellers look at me a little funny, like it's strange to meet a person who might be using their cells. Sometimes they see me as providing too much information, that I'm like one of the patients in those cheerful stock photographs on the walls of plasma centers coming to life and saying thanks. "Thanks" isn't quite right here, but neither is "Sorry our system is so exploitative you had to sell your blood."

When I talk to people about the plasma business, there's that last part that always seems to be a point of confusion: people are paid for their blood plasma, but not for whole blood. How did we come up with that little work-around? When America faces a shortage in its blood supplies, which are used for critical-care patients in hospitals and elsewhere, suggestions inevitably arise to pay people for whole blood to make up the difference. In all the research I've done over the years, what I've found is the United States has drawn this murky line, at best: patients generally are not paid for whole blood donations, while they *can* be paid for plasma in what is described as a token for their time. The World Health Organization and the U.S. Food and Drug Administration both argue that paid blood donations are less safe. Patients might be more inclined to lie about their medical history if they are looking for quick cash. But plasma and whole blood are both tested after they're drawn out of the body. In both cases, the companies that extract these fluids sell them to hospitals and other facilities.

A plasma donation does take longer than a blood donation, usually up to an hour in the chair for most people, not counting the wait time or the commute to and from the plasma center. Whole blood donations—the kind done at Red Cross stations—are much quicker. Also, in donating whole blood, there is no need to hook up the donor to a centrifuge to spin the blood into its parts and then infuse the cells back into their arm. Rather, it's a speedy extraction, a well-known process.

It seems the wholly arbitrary boundary we've set in the sand has kept blood donation to something seen as a noble, altruistic endeavor. Paid plasma, on the other hand, is often stigmatized by society, or ignored entirely. That explains why people who sell their plasma may be eager to discuss it in the abstract but not so keen to have their names associated with it. Many people I've interviewed have asked that I conceal their true identities. They don't want their family members to find out what they needed to do to get by. They don't want to have to justify their choices.

———

The social stigma attached to paid plasma donation, or lack of stigma in this place, is part of what makes Rexburg such an interesting spot to talk with people about selling plasma. It is a small city, home to about 35,000 people, roughly 95 percent of whom are members of the Mormon Church. Rexburg is also a college town, a busy hub for about 25,000 students at Brigham Young University–Idaho, a branch of the private college in Utah that's owned and run by the church. In an isolated city with a lot of college students, and, locals say, nowhere near enough part-time jobs to keep everyone paid for their work, shame about something as simple as selling plasma seems to go right out the window.

Rexburg is off the beaten path, even by standards of the Mountain West. It's a place you don't end up in by accident. An hour and a half from the west entrance to Yellowstone National Park and 30 minutes from bustling Idaho Falls, Rexburg is typical in the region as a town where not so long ago it was easy to live pretty well, cheaply. That's not so true anymore. Across the region, things are changing dramatically. Without the local wages keeping pace as the cost of everything goes up, people in towns across the West are doing what they must to make up the difference. In some places, if your body can tolerate it, that means selling blood plasma.

If you've heard the name Rexburg before, it might have been because of an infamous disappearance and murder case here that began to unfold in 2019. A woman named Lori Vallow and her partner, a man named Chad Daybell, were charged with murder after her two children went missing and their remains were found buried on Chad's property. Both of their former spouses had also died under shadowy circumstances shortly before Lori Vallow and Chad Daybell married. The investigation was still ongoing when I visited

Idaho. The couple was reportedly part of a Doomsday cult, departing from their lifelong Mormon beliefs and moving toward ideas about zombies and a select few chosen for the afterlife. The case, and the search for the missing children before they were found dead, made the headlines for months, with the events turned into catnip for the true-crime podcast and TV industry. It was the most intense attention Rexburg had drawn from the outside in years.

The Bees of the Hive

I turned off I-15 onto a two-lane highway that, twenty miles down the road, runs through sagebrush fields with the shark's-tooth outline of the Grand Tetons on the horizon until the highway melts into Rexburg's Main Street. I was making this trip only two days after a five-hour infusion of plasma-derived medication. My head was throbbing with that familiar IVIG hangover that I quell with endless coffee and liberal doses of ibuprofen. On this day, I was in a peculiar but familiar state of mind that follows nearly every one of my infusions—full of energy, almost manic, and not sleeping much.

The infusion drug itself contains nothing that should produce this effect, but it comes on so routinely after infusions that I can time when it will begin: nearly forty-eight hours after my drip has stopped. I have wondered whether it's just my body's reaction to the end of physical stress, or it's my own aggressive immune system brought to heel for another few weeks. Sometimes I let my mind wander to the notion that, while I'm infusing cells from thousands of other humans into my vein, I'm also capturing bursts of their energy, their life force. None of this makes any medical sense, and perhaps it's just the coffee, but it never feels like a caffeine buzz. It's more like euphoria.

The city was quiet and still, under a blanket of fresh snow and sparkling frost when I arrived. It sits in the shadow of a tall, gleaming white LDS Temple, with its hallmark golden trumpeting angel Moroni set atop a spire that watches over neat rows of newish, tidy homes and condos. Little indications all around tell you it's a Mormon town. There's the Deseret Bookstore, a faith-centered bookshop named for the state that the Mormon pioneers once hoped to create in the West. Inside a city park is the Beehive Pavilion. To the LDS faithful, the beehive image represents the religion's communal spirit;

the beehive remains to this day a state symbol that appears on high-way signs across Utah.

Mormonism has long dabbled with practices akin to socialism, such as living in collectives centered on group work, even though the church does not promote itself as such today. In the church's founding years, early members in the United Order sect lived communally and pooled resources; my long-dead Mormon pioneer ancestor was among them. So here, today, I wondered if the ideas of collectivism so prevalent in these parts are what helped make Rexburg an ideal place for the pharma giants to gather plasma. It has the bees of the hive, all rolling up their sleeves and being rewarded with prepaid debit cards for giving their essential cells to sick people in need. Cash fell out of favor long ago in the plasma business. Instead, a plasma seller earns money on their card, which is refilled each time they return and complete a donation—and it often comes with high bank fees to use.

On Rexburg's Facebook pages, the closest many small towns have to a community bulletin board, there is frequent talk of plasma donation and how to get the best deals. Social media like Facebook and Reddit has allowed plasma sellers to trade tips on making the most money and which clinics have the best-skilled technicians for easy needle sticks. I heard from one woman about a family that threw a party for their daughter's eighteenth birthday at a local plasma center, getting her in the door just as soon as she was old enough to begin making blood money. Paid plasma donation seems like a natural fit for this place.

Historically, multilevel marketing companies have been closely linked with Mormon communities, building their wealth from the personal networks of family and friends. Moms are encouraged in the Mormon faith to focus on their families and not work outside the home, so the plasma donations are a source of income without being an actual job—a chance to live the twin Mormon ideals of community service and contributing to the family pot, or just generating some personal spending money.

In Rexburg that day, I puzzled at the name of the pizza joint Righteous Slice, set on a corner within a larger building that also holds a plasma extraction center. Was it a play on surfer slang or a nod to the holy-minded? The odds are on the latter, given the vibe here. The town felt at once familiar and unlike what I'm used to seeing in the West. In any case, the plasma trade is booming so much in this little city that the plasma center near the college campus is the *second* one in town, a rare double-down for a place so small and relatively isolated.

Lurking Outside the Extraction Center

I figured the best way to find and interview plasma sellers was to lurk outside the extraction center and stop them when they left the center. I got some strange looks from passersby, but it was the only way to find a good cross-section of donors. Reddit, the internet discussion site, has plasma donor forums, but the chatter there is rarely hyper-local. Those posting comments tend to focus on which company pays best and what deals and bonuses plasma sellers can score in a given month, with a little dash of advice on what to eat and how to prepare. But I wanted to know *who* was selling plasma in Rexburg, so I needed to be here in person.

I suspected the companies that own these centers wouldn't like to have nosy interlopers, but Main Street in Rexburg is public property, so I had the right to be there. I parked near the corner, outside the Main Street plasma center, and began a routine to which I would grow accustomed in the following weeks and months.

The donors who exited the center didn't mind talking to me after I told them what I was up to. Several even seemed excited to meet a live person who might have used some of their plasma. There is something about a mostly Mormon town, in which everyone you meet seems a little bit like they work for the Chamber of Commerce—I felt a cheery, pro-Rexburg vibe pulsing through all our conversations.

Main Street in downtown Rexburg is standard-fare American West, dotted with brick storefronts and wooden buildings slowly being transformed from old businesses to new. It was bustling, even on a cold winter day. Cafés, bookstores, a cinema, and the police station line the central artery. But this was the first place I had seen a plasma center occupy prime real estate, in the middle of town. Right on a marquis corner of Main Street, in a repurposed grand brick structure known as the Charles Block, there's a big Grifols Biomat plasma clinic, with cookie-cutter advertisements in the window about getting paid to save lives. I've noticed the same kind of signs and banners on buildings and sidewalks from Texas to Michigan to Montana, but this was the first time I saw them planted on Main Street downtown. Usually, plasma extraction centers are built in out-of-the-way strip malls and on side streets, where rent is cheaper. They are rarely right in your face, on the main corner of a quaint business district.

When I returned to Rexburg later the following spring, it was warm and people wore short sleeves, so it was easier to spot the plasma donors. They strolled through downtown and across campus with tight blue elastic bandages wound around their elbows—a brigade of marked humans fueling some far-off companies in a global plasma industry. In all, on these visits, I spoke with a dozen people as they exited the buildings—seven men and five women. They were all white, which fits the demographics of Rexburg, a town whose population is 90 percent white. Of the dozen, nine were students, three were a bit older.

Two women in their forties left the center carrying their own blankets, which gave me a pang of familiarity. In the process of plasma donation, the extracted blood is spun through a machine to separate the plasma before returning the cells to the donor's body. The blood is cooled off while it's being mined for parts, so it is cool when reintroduced into the arm. A cold substance dripped into a vein for any length of time makes the donor cold, even on the warmest of days. As a similar recipient, I've grown fond of the down blankets I bring along for my treatments. Those plasma-selling women with their blankets had learned to do the same, at the other end of the production line.

Finding these little pieces of common experience made me feel a bit less weird as I lurked around out front to talk with people and ask them personal questions. I'm not just a journalist, extracting people's personal stories, I told myself; I'm also trying to solve a puzzle of my own. Later, when I went back in the spring, I watched a pair of older women in American flag T-shirts organize their knitting supplies in their tote bags before they opened the door to the center and went in. Something about their patriotic shirts crushed me a little bit, knowing the flag represents a country where selling body parts is normal.

In asking all these people for their personal stories, I found myself handling it almost as a survey, asking the same series of questions, then chatting with people a bit between their answers, helping them relax a bit into conversation. I went through the whys, the hows, the whens, and the whos. Most Rexburg donors told me they either heard about the plasma-selling practice when they got to college, or were referred to it by a friend, or had lived there long enough that they didn't quite remember not knowing about the center. It's one of those local places that has become ingrained in the culture, like a favorite café or the city park by the temple. Groups of students go together to sell plasma when they can, rendering the clinical aspect a little warmer, more social. I noticed people laughing at how ludicrous it all seemed when they started talking about why they were selling their plasma, like *Can you believe we have to do this?*

I asked one college student—a junior who didn't want to give his name—if he thought it was healthy to have his plasma drawn out for a long time, months or even years. This was on my checklist of questions in every place I visited. He paused for a moment and stared at me before answering, as though I'd pierced a barrier in his mind. When I mentioned that I use a medication made from plasma, it was an icebreaker that seemed to help him open up a little bit more. It was like we had a shared secret—but now we were talking about it out in the open, on a street corner. "I have no idea, but I think about that every time I'm here," he said, looking past me up the street.

None of the people I met on my two visits to Rexburg were first-timers at the plasma center, but the longest of them had been coming for less than a year. They sold plasma when they needed to and spent the money on necessities, for the most part. Rexburg is small, the job market is tight, and donating for cash is easy. That's what brought in Emily, a senior who was studying health sciences at BYU-Idaho. Her teeth chattered from the cold as we talked on the sidewalk. She told me that a part-time job would have taken too much time away from her studies, while selling plasma ate up only a couple of hours a week. She had been selling plasma for about three months and earning around $300 a month. For her, the money was enough and the pay seemed fair, even though the donation process could be a hassle. The worst part? For Emily, it was the needles. The stick isn't painful, exactly, but it's difficult to watch or think about.

She told me she does get tired on donation days, though, and the first time she sold plasma she passed out, right in the donation center. But she kept coming back, seeing it as a reliable way to earn money for groceries and other small items she needed while in school. Maybe, she said, she'd work at a plasma extraction center after she graduated.

That the practice is mostly innocuous is a message conveyed to donors by the plasma industry, and it is vastly understudied. Anecdotally, I've heard from multiple long-term plasma sellers that fatigue is a problem, sometimes to the point where they feel they might and do pass out, but it's almost always dismissed as not being a potential long-term health concern. Donors are told to eat better food with plenty of protein and drink lots of water, and they'll be fine. After all, the system wouldn't let them sell their plasma twice a week if it weren't safe, right? In truth, there are many lingering questions about what it does to people's bodies when they sell their plasma so often, or for so long, as the system encourages.

Long-Term Effects?

In a 2010 study, researchers found that the frequency of plasma extraction matters, and that the process leaves long-term donors with blood that has lower protein levels over time, as well as decreased levels of albumin and blood-borne immune particles. The study is unclear as to what impact this might have on the overall health of those who give plasma, but blood tests show unusually low levels in those building blocks of human function. The extraction industry does not, however, give its donors this precise information; in recent years it has started telling people who sell plasma to eat a protein-rich diet to keep up their health. Most of the plasma sellers I've met know that they need to eat protein to make up for what's lost in their extracted and reinjected cells.

The industry allows donors to give up to 104 times per year—even encouraging twice-a-week extraction by incentivizing multiple visits. For fourteen years, Xi Chen, a professor of global health at Yale University, studied health markers in thousands of plasma donors in China. As in the United States, the blood centers flourished in less wealthy parts of the country, where people were more open to selling plasma. Regulations have since curbed the trade, but his findings are compelling. Professor Xi described how long-term do-nors suffered fatigue and often needed to give up manual labor long before they were old enough to retire. In the United States, plasma donors have access to better nutrition, he said, and might not expe-rience the same kinds of health problems, because they are starting from a baseline of stronger bodies. But apart from this, there's little scientific evidence to tell us in great detail what happens to people who sell their plasma twice a week for years on end.

When I spoke with Dr. Xi about his research, I noticed on my desk a flyer that had come in the mail a few weeks before. It was from one of the big plasma companies, announcing a call for donors and hyping the extra cash for college. Because college students are a primary target for the plasma companies, especially those who go to large, public universities and live in towns like Missoula, I wasn't shocked, but it made my investigation feel more real. The practice of removing plasma to make medicines like mine is promoted to the public as harmless and helpful, but when it targets young peo-ple by turning their cells into commodities, can it be so? Dr. Xi told me that, after he published his research showing the potential harm to donors, several U.S. biopharmaceutical companies reached out to discuss his findings. He never responded.

In Rexburg, knowing all this, I was surprised when I asked Emily if she gets paid enough for her trouble and she answered yes without hesitation. It was a pretty quick and easy way for her to fill the gap in her budget, even though she has felt ill from doing it.

————

There was a pragmatism about it all that seemed to pervade the at-titude of most students I spoke with in Rexburg—that selling their plasma was a fair way to make money when they didn't have a lot of other options. A small city like this one doesn't have enough part-time jobs for thousands of students, and the jobs that do exist get filled fast. Selling plasma can be a more reliable way for a lot of students to earn extra money while they're in school. But COVID-19 saw the Rexburg college students' plasma-selling largesse take a darker turn.

CHAPTER 4
The Blood of Our Youth

BYU-Idaho is deeply troubled by accounts of individuals
who have intentionally exposed themselves or others to COVID-19,
with the hope of getting the disease and being paid for plasma
that contains COVID-19 antibodies.
—BYU-Idaho administration

The first fall surge of the COVID-19 pandemic, starting in October 2020, saw Rexburg's easygoing, even eager attitude toward donating blood plasma for pay veer into the surreal and dangerous. This was months before vaccines to protect against the virus were developed and became widely available. For many people, including myself, getting COVID might have been a death sentence during the pandemic's early grip. It was during those days that Brigham Young University–Idaho, the Mormon-run college around which Rexburg is organized, sent out that stern and peculiar warning to its entire student body.

The notice went on to warn that spikes in COVID cases on campus were pushing the college to consider all-remote learning to keep its students, staff, and faculty safe. This was a decision the school had tried to avoid, but the significant, even more troubling news was that college students might have been trying to get COVID on purpose. The notice concluded by offering help: "BYU-Idaho recognizes that, for many in our campus community, the physical, emotional, and financial strain of this pandemic is very real. If students are struggling, BYU-Idaho stands ready to help. There is never a need to resort to behavior that endangers health or safety in order to make ends meet."

Rexburg is many things. It's very Mormon, very white, very tidy. It's an outlying town close to Yellowstone National Park, so it gets some tourist traffic. It's in the rapidly changing Mountain West. But first and foremost, it's a college town. This is the city the LDS faithful in Idaho and beyond trust to educate their children after high school. The businesses, from bookstores to fast-food places to cookie shops, embrace Mormon youth culture. And so do the plasma centers.

In the months after the college's warning went out, I spoke with multiple people in Rexburg and beyond, trying to track down the incident that prompted the university officials to issue that alarming message. The college administration itself—rarely an open book when it comes to explaining anything—never responded to my inquiries. But it was for some time the talk of the town and the subject of multiple national news stories. There has never been a verified report of students deliberately trying to catch COVID. Still, nearly everyone I talked to said it was entirely plausible, but they couldn't point me to anyone who actually did it.

The reasoning was easy to understand: blood plasma containing COVID antibodies, taken from a person who had contracted the virus and survived, paid more than a regular plasma donation. At the time, young people were in the lowest risk group for severe complications if they contracted the disease. For some people of college age, COVID-19 sparked horror, but for many more in that cohort the illness came on like a mild flu or presented no symptoms at all. The overarching message conveyed to the public by state and federal governments desperate to encourage people to continue to work was, in short, "If you're young and healthy, you'll be fine." College students and people in their twenties and thirties took that advice, as evidenced by their lower vaccination rates when the lifesaving shots became available. By December of 2021, when COVID vaccines were widely offered to American adults of all ages, 75 percent of the people who remained unvaccinated were under the age of 50.

In one of the more naked instances of American medical capitalism, the COVID-19 pandemic ignited a brief boom, then a bust, in the blood plasma industry. In Rexburg, where students might have made $45 to $50 from a single, one-off plasma donation in normal times, they could now make $100 for a single post-COVID plasma draw. In other parts of the country, some extraction centers offered recovered COVID patients much higher rates, even for a onetime plasma donation. To be clear, some nonprofit blood organizations did spring up in the middle of the crisis to collect the plasma of survivors, who were unpaid, and they placed the plasma in the pool for experimentation. Across the country, including in Rexburg, pay rates went up for plasma from people who'd had COVID.

"I would not be surprised if that was some of the thinking for some students," suggested Rett Nelson, the eastern Idaho journalist I talked with about Rexburg. "It's an easy way to make money. You go and sit for an hour."

Most of the Rexburg plasma sellers, especially the students, whom I asked about COVID plasma laughed nervously and answered cautiously, as though I might be trying to catch them doing something wrong. They never quite told me they knew the COVID story to be the truth, but they were all making money at the plasma center, and they said it was something people would consider doing if the payout were to become higher than a normal donation.

The rates for plasma sellers have gone up quite a bit since Rett Nelson graduated in 2012, but then again so has the cost of most other things, from gas to rent. Students who need to make money might think it's no big deal to catch COVID once to earn a bigger payout for their plasma. After all, if the primary goal is to make money, why not take what has been presented as a minor risk to catch a virus that makes you even more money in the process? "People do all sorts of crazy things for money," one BYU-Idaho student told me with a laugh. I couldn't argue with his point.

The Virus Meets the Crisis

This little saga began when the United States, in a mad hunt for tools to fight the pandemic, started throwing ideas and money at the wall to see what might work. In the first year of the pandemic, desperate for effective treatments but lacking the will or foresight to organize simple systemic measures like widespread availability of free testing, masks, and robust contract tracing, the federal government invested $800 million in something called "convalescent plasma." The theory behind the massive experiment goes like this: Survivors of the illness carry antibodies in their blood, the effect of successfully fighting the COVID virus, and those antibodies protect them for some time from a subsequent infection. Transferring those antibodies to other people via plasma infusions might help vulnerable patients fight the infection—theoretically like adding another line of defense to one's immune system.

It's a notion that's been around for more than a century, with some moderate documented success against infections from some viruses. In 1901, German scientist Emil Adolf von Behring became the first winner of the Nobel Prize in Physiology or Medicine for his work on "serum theory." His research centered on exposing horses, goats, and guinea pigs to diphtheria, then treating them with the antibody-rich blood of animals recovered from that illness, with some degree of success. Scientists believed this body of research paved the way to what in hindsight looks like a different form of immunization, passing the protective elements contained in the blood of one animal to the blood of another to battle illness. Over the years, through disease outbreaks including the 1918 flu pandemic and the Ebola virus nearly 100 years later, antibody-rich blood has been collected from survivors and transfused into suffering patients to help ward off deadly consequences.

Whether this idea worked for COVID-19 is still a matter of debate, though studies do show some potential. It wasn't an entirely demented idea dreamed up by the Trump administration, but neither was it a likely solution. A 2006 meta-study of patients during the 1918 influenza showed that plasma treatment may have reduced mortality among the sick who had received it. Similar studies throughout the years have showed mixed results, but success does appear to hinge on which type of disease the antibodies are working against. In our modern era, in a world where billions are spent on biopharmaceutical research, the United States reached back a century to a seemingly archaic solution, and it enlisted the help of corporations to make it happen.

In 2020, in spite of the skepticism of much of the global scientific community, the U.S. Food and Drug Administration gave emergency authorization for the treatment of COVID-19 with convalescent blood plasma—the plasma of people who had been infected with COVID. The same profit-making companies that were positioned to collect the giant pool of plasma to use for existing diseases, like mine, jumped in with gusto and received a whole lot of funding. People who had recovered from the coronavirus were being offered big cash payouts for donating their antibody-rich plasma.

The plasma was used in research, including clinical trials to determine whether the golden fluid would reduce mortality and diminish the seriousness of the illness. By December of 2021, the grand experiment, touted by former U.S. president Donald Trump (the man who spectacularly bungled the COVID response from the first day and who off-handedly suggested that sunlight and bleach injections could rid a person of the virus) had flopped. The World Health Organization warned against using convalescent plasma for COVID, saying, "There was no clear benefit for critical outcomes such as mortality and mechanical ventilation for patients with non-severe, severe or critical illness, and significant resource requirements in terms of cost and time for administration." By then, the FDA had also issued its own caution, saying that the grand plasma experiment did not appear to have any strong, predictable results in treating COVID symptoms.

Some of the COVID blood plasma efforts were a bit shadier than others, a bit more nakedly obvious money grabs based on bad science. The Associated Press reported in November 2020 that a well-connected Republican political donor, running a plasma company out of his condo in South Carolina and who had no manufacturing capabilities, was in line to receive as much as $65 million in federal money to ramp up a convalescent plasma production facility. Indeed, massive federal funding for a plasma center that didn't exist was the peak American COVID response. The U.S. government turned over large portions of the pandemic response, from testing to treatment, to private industry, with its flops and stalls along the way, so why not do the same with convalescent plasma? The AP article summed up the South Carolina mess: "The story of how a tiny business that exists only on paper has managed to snare attention from the highest reaches of the U.S. military and government is emblematic of the Trump administration's frenetic response to the coronavirus pandemic."

The South Carolina debacle was only one piece of the government's scattershot approach to pandemic plasma. In a year, the federal government distributed 722,000 units of convalescent plasma across the country to health-care facilities. Yet study after study showed it had little effect against COVID. It had done next to nothing. While Americans scrambled for coherent government guidance in a confused mess guided mainly by the politics of state governments, and many shunned vaccines in part due to a lack of solid outreach and public health messaging, a new sea of human plasma was collected from people who had been ill.

"We were hoping that the use of COVID-19 convalescent plasma would achieve at least a 10% reduction in disease progression in [a high-risk] group, but instead the reduction we observed was less than 2%," remarked principal researcher Clifton Callaway, MD, PhD, from the University of Pittsburgh, about findings reported in the *New England Journal of Medicine*. "That was surprising to us. As physicians, we wanted this to make a big difference in reducing severe illness and it did not."

The Higher Education Trap

In the spring of 2022, I returned to Rexburg to talk with more plasma sellers. On the sidewalk near the extraction site near the campus, I approached Boden, a 22-year-old wearing a gray graphic T-shirt, the telltale blue elastic bandage concealing a newly mined hole in the crook of his left arm. "Did you just donate plasma?" I asked.

"Well, technically, yes," he said, looking confused at why I wanted to know. I explained that I was a journalist writing about the reasons people do this, and he started talking a mile a minute, smiling in the bright sun. Boden had just graduated with a degree in accounting, and he said that finding work in his field in Rexburg, or work in any field, was tough. His wife heard about making money by selling plasma, and while her protein levels were too low to continue doing it herself, it had given him no health problems. Twice a week for the last year, he returned to the extraction clinic and had his plasma drawn out and his prepaid debit card topped up. When I asked him about the potential stigma of selling plasma, he looked at me with a blank stare and said, "What do you mean, stigma?" He was genuinely puzzled. In his world, in Rexburg, it was not so much of a worry.

The only part of the process that bothered Boden was the needle—he couldn't watch when they put it in his arm. I know this feeling myself and have never watched any of the hundreds of needle sticks I've had over the years. Other than that, he had a few tests that showed he needed more protein, so he made sure to eat a lot of meat, or eggs, to keep on track. He was physically fit, young, and thought the pay was enough for the amount of time and hassle it required of him. He didn't see a problem, as long as he kept his protein levels up.

Rexburg might be an unusual place, but it's by no means an anomaly. It's a microcosm of one aspect of America's plasma economy—the higher education trap. Companies that buy and sell blood plasma know college students need money, that jobs are difficult to find and maintain when students are in school full-time, so for younger, healthy people, donations can account for easy money. The industry appears to understand this well and geotargets many of its extraction centers in college towns.

My map of plasma centers around the country has red dots at cities and towns with big public universities, like Ann Arbor, Michigan, and Madison, Wisconsin, and Ames, Iowa. The blood trade comes with advertising that's specifically designed to bring in college students, with flyers and billboards featuring smiling young people extolling the virtues of easy money for textbooks or spring break while helping to save lives at the same time. Any college student in the country who isn't rich has probably heard of selling plasma to make ends meet, and many have tried it. Several of the students I met brought up the rising cost of housing as a concern that drove them to selling their plasma. After all, it's expensive to live in Idaho these days on a local income, even in this little city.

I asked the students I met outside of Rexburg's plasma centers whether they would continue selling their plasma after they left college. The answers were split. Some wanted to stop as soon as they could; others thought it would be a good way to supplement their income. For Boden, who was planning to move soon to Meridian, Idaho, with his wife to live with her family, it meant looking for another place to continue selling. But Meridian is a smaller town, with no college and no plasma center. The nearest is probably thirty minutes' drive away. The geotargeting of plasma extraction leaves a lot of people out and maintains it as something people do while in school. A look at the economics of getting a college degree can help explain why.

In the thirty years leading up to the present, the average cost of college tuition in America has tripled, landing at the high end at more than $35,000 a year for private colleges. And that's not counting accompanying living expenses, which can add another $20,000 a year for each student, according to the Education Data Initiative. The tuition and living costs vary widely, of course, but the expectation of students to go to college has risen and so has the debt that so many take on to make that happen. In the empty space where government funding should be, plasma extraction has materialized as a Band-Aid for many students.

Along with the untenable rise in the cost of higher education, student debt has soared. In my wider survey of plasma donors around the country, I heard from people who have used blood plasma money to help pay down their student debt. In essence, these loans have saddled entire generations of students with payments the size of what their parents and grandparents might have spent buying a house and a nice car. By some estimates, student loans typically take twenty years to pay off.

The U.S. government has has taken some initial steps toward student debt relief and limiting untenable loan payments. Even that ignited a fight over extending grace to the "wrong" people who have too much money—those who come from wealthy families or earn above a certain income level after college. We are a rich yet incredibly stingy country especially when it comes to extending a hand to those in need. State and private universities continue to raise their tuition, the cost of living is on the rise across the land, and so plasma often flows from students' bodies to fill the financial gaps.

Looking back through recent history, the American culture of young people selling pieces of themselves, literally, is not new or wholly confined to blood. Even when I was in college in the 1990s, I knew students who sold parts of themselves to pay for what they needed. One of my roommates was paid to be a sperm donor; a friend enrolled in every campus clinical trial possible, making $40 or $50 for each. Paid plasma wasn't an option in my city back then, but I heard about women selling their eggs, a prospect I found both intriguing and horrifying.

Diane Tober, a medical anthropologist at the University of California, San Francisco, has investigated the reasons women sell their eggs. Tober conducted interviews and surveys involving more than 600 egg donors, and she found that, in the United States, college debt is a leading reason women undertake this process. Contrary to the soothing stock imagery and easy moneymaking opportunities advertised, egg donation is a complex and invasive procedure involving intensive hormone therapy. It does pay women generously if they participate in multiple cycles. But especially if repeated, the practice can have serious, long-term health consequences. A piece Tober wrote for *Salon* aligned with what I heard from plasma sellers:

> The United States emerges in my study as the only country where women in their 20s feel compelled to make medical decisions with life-long implications to reduce or eliminate the affliction of student debt. Without this burden people may still decide to donate eggs for financial relief—even in countries like Spain where donor compensation is much lower than in the US—but they are not driven by the same financial desperation arising from the cost of education.

We demand that young people go to college to get the jobs that will lead them into comfortable lives, but the years of higher education themselves are increasingly difficult for most people to navigate financially. Tuition, rent, gas, and food—the basic essentials of life while in school, not even counting money for fun—have reached record highs and there's been little effort made in most communities to alleviate these burdens. This paradox forces students to make difficult and too-soon decisions about their wealth, finances, health, and bodies.

Much of the mainstream discussion about higher education in America centers on a few wealthy private colleges where many of the students come from affluent families. I have long believed this fascination with the Ivy League and expensive private colleges stems from the fact that the people who run for national office and who write for the national media have attended those schools in outsized numbers compared with the rest of the population. Many of their children strive for the same schools and careers. They see what they are used to seeing and talk about who and what they know best. Many of them have never met someone who sells plasma to eke out a living. They might not know how students at public universities use the plasma money to make the rent. But in the rest of the country, in pockets like Rexburg and across cities and states less wealthy, students are selling their body parts to pay for their education.

At BYU-Idaho in Rexburg, tuition is much lower than the national average—less than $5,000 per year. The university is deliberately affordable. Many of its students come from rural parts of the Mountain West, where family incomes are lower than in other regions of the country, and whatever extra money students can earn for meeting their living expenses is welcomed.

Among the students I interviewed outside the plasma center in Rexburg, most said they use the money for rent, gas, or groceries. Tuition itself isn't the issue; their blood money goes toward the price of living. The median household income in Rexburg is less than half the national average—about $31,000 a year here, compared with $67,000 nationally. This persistent wedge of income disparity helps to explain why a city so small has two thriving paid plasma extraction centers.

On the front window of the Grifols Biomat right near the BYU-Idaho campus, a large sign spells out for students how much they can make by selling their plasma every month:

DONOR PAYMENTS
1st donation $25
2nd donation $30
3rd donation $35
4th donation $40
5th donation $75
6th donation $75
7th donation $75
8th donation $100
9th donation $100
10th donation $100

Total in 9 donations: $555
Total in 10 donations: $655

Below this schedule in the window is the schedule for new donors, for the first month they sign up, who make $100 each time. It's a lure to pull them into the system and get them hooked on blood money. I can't help but think back to the dystopian plasma economy slogans of China, urging farmers who were poor to offer up their veins to be tapped in exchange for promises of potential wealth: "Stick out an arm, show a vein, open your hand, and make a fist, 50 kuai." Or, "If you want a comfortable standard of living, go sell your plasma," and "To give plasma is an honor." It seemed ludicrous in China; it feels the same here.

———

At the plasma center just off campus in Rexburg, I met a few students who showed up twice a week to make the maximum amount of money. Across from a fancy chain cookie store, I stood on the sidewalk and caught plasma sellers as they left the building. Many of them did not want to use their real names in print, but they seemed happy enough to talk about it.

I asked a person I'll call Paul, a junior at the college, if he was embarrassed to tell people he sold his plasma. He looked at me like I wasn't that smart. No, he'd never thought to be ashamed of it. That's because nobody cared if you sold plasma in Rexburg. "It's just what we do," he said. The downside was that if he got bounced from donating for some reason—or if he missed a week for any reason—he had to start all over again. He referred his friends to the center as new donors so as to get bonus money whenever he could. I asked if he ever got sick from the process, and he said no, but his girlfriend had to quit after only two donations because it made her too tired to function the rest of the day.

I've noticed this divide repeatedly. Some plasma donors don't notice anything but the hassle of time and needles, while others can't get past the crushing fatigue. I've spoken with several scientists about the health impacts, and the main concern is the frequency of plasma donation in the United States. To refill that giant pool, companies do what they can to draw donors in twice a week, every week, for as long as possible. We are the only country in the world that allows people to donate their plasma so often. And even though formal studies have not linked serious health problems with long-term donors yet, the rush and demand for plasma as much as twice a week does raise questions. The fatigue, the nausea, the chills—they are all aftereffects.

The plasma industry insists it is not exploiting people, that payment schemes are, technically, only tokens of appreciation for donors who give their time. But the business has built a deliberately complex pyramid of payments and incentives designed to draw people and keep them in the system. The reality of the plasma economy tells an entirely different story from the one the industry wants to present. In college towns like Rexburg, a steady stream of willing raw material is derived from a large part of the population who are willing and need money.

Nobody gets rich selling their blood plasma. They get by, barely, or get a little closer to being able to afford some of the things that bring them some joy. Though the industry maintains that its payment schedule is to compensate donors for their time, that donation time doesn't increase with each donation. Rather, the payment schedules are clearly designed to pull people in as often as possible to make the maximum amount of money. More specifically, in Rexburg, a person who never misses twice-weekly donations can make more than $7,000 a year—a healthy income for a college student in a town with a high rate of poverty. If you've already made seven donations in a month, why not up your income just by adding one more trip to the plasma center? This is how the companies keep people returning, even when the crushing schedule feels like too much for their bodies to handle. In essence, the payment structure punishes those who don't come as often.

———

I left Rexburg after two days of chats with students on the street corner and drove back through the mountains to Montana, all the while thinking about the trap that is higher education. The students I met were focused on getting a degree, graduating, and moving into middle-class jobs. But to get there, they had to sell pieces of their bodies. Some of them may even have tried to contract a potentially deadly virus to make a little more money than usual. On the sidewalk in downtown Rexburg, the donors I told about my reliance on plasma seemed glad to meet a person who benefited from their donations. They were used to seeing people like me only in the centers' glossy posters and brochures. But I couldn't shake the feeling that this was all quite wrong, and that hooking college students into an endless cycle of selling their pieces shouldn't be the normal way of our world. Most people I talked with in Rexburg seemed happy to be seen, to know that someone was interested in learning about why they needed to do what they were doing. For now, I decided, that's what I could do. I was still trying to figure out how exploitative this industry actually is, but it seemed hearing the plasma sellers' stories was an essential step. Next, I wanted to know how we got to this point, and so I dove into the sometimes-unsavory history of extracting and transferring human blood.

CHAPTER 5
Moving Blood

Blood is that fragile scarlet tree
we carry within us.
—Osbert Sitwell

The Museum of the History of Medicine in Paris is not a place for the faint of heart. Hidden away on the second floor of one of the grand white marble buildings on the campus of Descartes University, the tourists who'd otherwise flock to the French capital for the likes of the Louvre and Musée d'Orsay are not likely to find themselves lost in this carnival of the macabre. After only a few moments inside the main room, I'm enthralled by all the . . . *weird* on display. The university's medical history collection includes one of the oldest and largest displays of surgical equipment from eras long past, when the practice was cruder and constantly evolving, along with tools that were used to perform Napoleon's autopsy. There are centuries-old instruments once used to extract and transfuse blood, along with cutting and carving tools for human flesh and bone. Two stories of an airy, large room contain a vast assemblage of blunt instruments that tell a tale of the pain and suffering that built the modern science of medicine.

And then there is the showpiece, an ornamental table built and adorned, for wholly unclear reasons, with human body parts. I read about the table before visiting the museum, so I knew to look for it. Otherwise, I'd have mistaken it for an ornate piece of museum furniture. A card on the table's round glass top explains the bizarre ornament, given as a gift in 1866: "Made by Efisio Marini, Italian naturalist doctor, and offered to Napoléon III. This table is formed of petrified brains, blood, bile, liver, lungs and glands upon which rests a foot, four ears and sections of vertebrae, which are also petrified."

I was intrigued by the sideshow of forgotten gore, but that wasn't why I had come here, stopping at the morbid museum with a friend while on a brief trip to the French capital. It's a painting I was looking for in this place, and I finally found it hanging just outside the entryway to the museum; its location was almost a physical cue that the story it told was too strange and ugly to be part of a collection that proudly showcases a table made from actual parts of people's bodies. Because the painting was physically separate from the collection, it took me a while to find. I didn't spot it until I turned to face the door as we got ready to leave.

There, hanging above the staircase, was a scene I found stranger than the disembodied body-parts table. A young woman dressed in white lay prone across the canvas, her face ashen with illness. Standing over her, a doctor focused on inserting a long needle into the vein in the cleave of her left arm as blood trickled out. Behind them, on a second table, lay a goat. Four men in suits and butchers' aprons surrounded them, holding the animal and monitoring devices. The goat had been partly butchered but appeared still alive, a tube running from its severed neck toward the young woman.

Transfusion de sang du chèvre (*Transfusion of a Goat's Blood*), painted in 1892 by French artist Jules Adler, might seem the work of grotesque imagination. But it's a piece commissioned by a Paris physician, Samuel Bernheim, who became widely known for treating tuberculosis patients. The painting shows a real moment, captured to mark Bernheim's publication of an article in a French medical journal about a novel treatment for the respiratory illness. Bernheim recommended not a full transfusion but, rather, a small dose of 150 to 200 grams of goat's blood, infused into the veins of women suffering from TB. Women, by the doctor's assessment, were physiologically more like animals than men.

Bernheim, who was 37 at the time, paid the painter 1,200 francs to capture the moment that would highlight what he believed would be a medical breakthrough in treating what was then one of the world's deadliest diseases. His experiment was off the mark, even for its time. Animal-to-human transfusion attempts, too often deadly for the human patients, had fallen out of favor after causing a stir in the 1600s. When Bernheim had his moment immortalized on canvas, there was little attention paid to the practice, as it didn't work. By the time Bernheim's article appeared, the painting was already a relic of a practice shunned and considered barbaric by most.

Our Dear Elixir

Our enduring fascination with moving blood from person to person runs long through recorded history. Humans for centuries have been convinced that blood is the elixir of life, the fountain of youth, the substance that can repair the ravages of time and violence. The experiments that moved blood from one body to another often involved transferring the blood of people who had less power in society into the bodies of people who were wealthier and more powerful. Early blood transfusions in Europe often drew from the poor and the mentally ill. Even when the practice failed, which it did, repeatedly, true believers in the power of human blood insisted on continuing. The history of medicine is riddled with exploitation, with experiments on people who were not of the moneyed classes, and of using the results of those practices to build a science that served wealth and status.

The record of modern humankind is crowded with tales of wealthy and powerful men, and a few women, who tried to reverse time and cheat death by devouring the blood of the young, in innumerable ways. In fifteenth-century Rome, Pope Innocent VIII was given fresh blood from three 10-year-old boys, in an attempt to rouse him from a coma in the aftermath of a stroke. Both he and the boys died. And then there was Hungarian countess Elizabeth Bathory, whose purported serial killings possibly inspired the legend of Count Dracula. She may have murdered young girls so she could fight her own aging by bathing in their blood.

A German doctor proposed young-blood transfusions in the seventeenth century, and the advances in blood science by London's Royal Society were made partly in quest of the same. Also, there was

Alexander Bogdanov in Russia in the 1920s, a Bolshevik who experimented with young-blood infusions on himself and on a small circle of fellow intellectuals, including Lenin's sister. He claimed the transfusions had repaired his eyesight and softened his wrinkles, but the tonic eventually killed him when he took an infusion from a student whose blood was infected with both tuberculosis and malaria.

It was hard to be at the Paris gore museum and not think of the people I had met who sold their blood plasma. The science is proven, and I don't believe what they are doing poses an immediate or severe risk to their health. But why have we decided that the blood of the working poor in the United States should feed a massive, profit-motivated global industry?

Bloody tales throughout human history often go hand in glove with creating cures for wealthy and powerful eccentrics. Yet, in many cases, the stories are impossible to verify. Case in point: North Korea's late, deeply secretive dictator Kim Jong Il was stalked by rumors that he injected himself with the blood of young virgins to keep himself youthful and vibrant. Whether this worked for him is debatable, to put it mildly. But wealthy and powerful men have long sought the blood and life of the young and beautiful. Even though today's experiments, like one high-profile endeavor to instill youth through infusing blood plasma from young people into older bodies, have failed, it seems we won't stop trying to find ways to use blood as a fountain of youth. For thousands of people like me, whose immune systems fail or malfunction, other people's blood is an elixir. I wasn't sure how to feel about that, so I kept reading about blood in human history.

––––––

It is generally acknowledged that the first successful blood transfusion was in 1665, when a British doctor kept dogs alive by giving them blood from other dogs. It wasn't until 150 years later, however, that the practice worked in humans. Another British doctor, James Blundell, used human blood transfusions to treat women who hemorrhaged during childbirth. That innovation changed the world of modern medicine and led to a period of furious scientific discoveries about blood, including the revolution that came in 1901. That year, an Austrian doctor, Karl Landsteiner, identified the three human blood groups—a revolutionary step in determining whose blood could be moved to whom.

Research during World War II involving wounded soldiers on the battlefield led to the innovations that changed my own life. Scientists developed the fractionation machine, which separates plasma—the protein liquid part of blood—from the red blood cells. This one innovation initiated a whole world of medicines that would be developed in the following years.

Plasma is universal; there is no need to match donor and recipient blood types in moving the fluid from one person to another for medical purposes. The plasma contains antibodies and other attributes, but it is absent red blood cells. It can, in emergencies, be used to save lives.

This period of blood discovery moved fast. In a few short years, scientists in the UK and the United States developed tools and practices that allowed blood to be separated into its parts so as to make critical medications, as well as the devices needed to dry and store plasma for long periods. The advances came in the name of saving soldiers' lives but they also led to a shift in medical practices that remains with us today.

A doctor named Ogden Carr Bruton, head of pediatrics at Walter Reed Medical Center in Washington, D.C., is credited with the first use of human immunoglobulin made from plasma, which he injected under the skin of a child to treat an immune system disorder. From there, a series of doctors and medical researchers began experimenting with and using immune particles extracted from plasma to treat a host of problems with the immune system. By the 1970s, human intravenous immunoglobulin, or IVIG, became a mass-produced drug, if one used sparingly and often limited to life-threatening situations. It wouldn't become standard treatment for diseases like mine until well into the 2000s, when the blood markets of America mushroomed and the engines of paid-plasma extraction revved up.

Today, the plasma extracted from millions in America is spun into drugs used for immune deficiencies, respiratory diseases, hemophilia, neurological conditions (like mine), and other blood disorders. Medicine made from plasma is also used in cardiac surgery, burn treatments, and blood disorders in infants. In court filings, the plasma industry has also described research with plasma-borne treatments for Alzheimer's, Parkinson's and liver disease, as well as transplants and heart disease. Its uses are many, and drug companies are looking for even more.

My Journey in Blood

I was 25 or 26 when my body first turned on itself. It started slowly, almost imperceptibly. First, my fingers began to tingle and go numb, which continued over the course of a few months. Then the numbness crept into my toes and feet, crawling up my ankles and calves. In the beginning, I saw several doctors to try to figure out what was going on. They only saw a healthy young woman and didn't spend much time trying to find what was wrong. It was nothing; it might be something. It could be multiple sclerosis; it might be a repetitive motion injury in my hands from sitting long hours at the keyboard because I was a journalist. None of this made much sense, and as the symptoms grew worse in my body, I began to think it might always be this way.

When I could no longer walk up the single flight of stairs in my apartment building to do my laundry, I finally arranged an appointment with a neurologist. He conducted a physical exam, nodding along as I told him about my weird symptoms that had grown worse during the year. But he ordered no tests, no scans, not even simple blood work. Instead, he told me it was all in my head. An anxiety disorder was causing my problems; the physical manifestations in my hands and feet were likely all imagined, products of a brain doing too much thinking. There was nothing wrong with me but a little lousy brain chemistry that could easily be corrected with the proper medication. He wrote me a prescription for an antidepressant, Zoloft, and sent me on my way.

That someone paid to specialize in neurological diseases dismissed a significant disease sitting right in front of him still boggles my mind. But this is the way of doctors dealing with women, especially young women, in distress. Our problems are routinely diminished and dismissed. Even serious, life-threatening diseases are ignored in favor of a diagnosis that amounts to "hysteria." It's pretty clear to me now that this is what happened in my twenties, but as I look back on it, I'm not so sure it mattered. That dismissive doctor allowed me a few more years to pretend that I was fine. In all honesty, he shouldn't have been treating patients, but at the same time I leaned into the delusion he gave me. Catching the real problem earlier would not have made much difference in terms of the progression of the disease; it wasn't going to kill me. I was luckier than some other women who have been through this same experience.

I did get better, for a little while. The antidepressant, also a treatment for anxiety, began to work and it calmed my panic attacks. The truth was that I was indeed anxious. My hands and feet were going numb, weird pains shot through my limbs when I slept, and I walked with the clumsy gait of someone sixty years my senior. But I had seen a brain and nerve doctor. Because he told me it was all in my head, he was easier to believe than what I knew: that there was something wrong in other parts of my body. The symptoms of that first wave eventually receded; I know now that it was a period of remission. Whatever caused my cells to attack the nerves in my limbs had settled down for a while. I slowly regained my ability to do most of what I used to do, and I decided I didn't need to know any more.

Denial is enticing when you face the possibility of a chronic illness. I was lucky and I was in good health otherwise. My body overcame the traces of that first attack, and I resumed a mostly normal life, marveling at how I had been told what was inside my head could have manifested itself in such a physical way across the rest of my body. Deep down, of course, I knew that wasn't true.

The disease came roaring back a few years later. I was approaching 30, still working as a state capital reporter in Montana, when my body began to fall apart again. The antidepressant no longer worked on the anxiety that took over when my hands and feet went numb. For months, it felt like I'd crossed my legs and both had fallen asleep. It was the same with my hands. This may sound like a mild annoyance, but think about trying to stand up when your legs are crossed too long and one has gone numb. It doesn't work quite right. When my body is attacking itself, the sensation is constant and the numbness is disabling.

After years of pretending this was normal, I finally found a different doctor, who saw that it wasn't all in my head. During a physical exam, he noticed the muscle in the arch of my foot, which twitched incessantly. From that, he could see there was likely a problem with the nerves that sent signals from my brain to my muscles. He ran a series of tests, including one that involved attaching electrodes to either end of a nerve and then having a machine send electric impulses across the wire to measure how fast they travel. My nerves were shot, but I had managed to cover that up so well that I could walk normally. But the test readings were so bad, so slow, that the doctor put the electrodes on his own inner arm to make sure the measuring device was working.

There were more tests, then, to rule out illnesses. An MRI, a spinal tap, the long needles piercing skin and muscle in the small of my back to draw fluid from my spinal cord and be checked for a certain protein marker. There were countless blood tests and pinpricks to determine how much sensation I had in my limbs. At each doctor's visit, there was a little device that reminded me of a pizza slicer. The doctor would run the wheel up and down my ankles and wrists, asking me to describe where the numbness began and where it ended.

As the doctor watched, I walked across rooms, trying, and often failing, to stand on my toes—too many times to count. In the end, like most medical diagnoses it was a process of elimination. I came away with a diagnosis of chronic inflammatory demyelinating polyneuropathy—a disease so rare that its name is only a description of what it does, not its cause.

Researchers' best guess is that my immune system mistakes some of the covering of my nerves as a foreign invader and attacks healthy cells that deliver my brain's messages to the muscles. The result is a bundle of messed-up wires. The attack never launches in my brain itself, just in the outer tendrils of the nervous system—the peripheral nerves. The disease has more well-known, more common cousins, but this specific form affects roughly 5 people in every 100,000, or about 550,000 people worldwide.

Even the precise numbers are hard to pin down. It is odd, rare, and, though extremely annoying and potentially disabling, manageable. Therefore, it's not a disease given to large funding or study efforts by drug companies, which prefer to focus on the more common diseases where developed cures promise greater profits. And yet what I now know is that the main treatment for my disease brings profits to a global business, one that relies upon the unsteadiness of America's fragmented and depleted social safety net.

When I was first diagnosed with this odd disease, the doctor prescribed a course of steroids. Back then, that was the standard first-line treatment for illnesses like mine. Prednisone is an unpleasant drug. I was on it only for a few months, but what I remember is that it made me feel like crawling out of my skin. I was not exactly angry, just annoyed a lot of the time. As far as I could tell, it didn't do much to fix the numbness in my hands and feet, but it made me an anxious person to be around.

By the time I quit taking steroids, the disease had again begun going into remission on its own, which happens with no explanation. The doctor told me if the symptoms returned, we would try a different tactic next time: either a process called plasmapheresis, whereby your blood is removed from your body and spun around in a machine—something I still don't understand—or a drug made from human plasma—at that time a promising advancement in the treatment of certain immune-system maladies like mine. This being America, most doctors even then—the early 2000s—knew that IVIG was the best available treatment. It was also extremely expensive—as much as $100,000 a year for repeated treatments—and often was not covered by health insurance programs.

The decision on how to battle another attack would likely depend on how good my health insurance was. Being diagnosed young, before the U.S. health insurance system had grown even worse with its additional costs and frequent denials of coverage, has helped me weather the disease as much as anything else. Knowing the potential costs of treatment without insurance, I've made health insurance a top priority and have never gone a day without it. I realize this, too, is a privilege; many people in my situation are too ill or disabled to work enough to cover the costs and copays that come with private insurance.

If you met me in person, you would not be able to tell anything was wrong with me. I know because people have a habit of telling me exactly this when they find out there *is* something wrong with me. I've hidden my condition from most people deliberately, telling only my closest friends and family through the years. The stigma and marginalization that accompany chronic illness, especially in the United

States, are so threaded through all facets of life that I don't talk about it with people I don't trust. I know about employment discrimination; I'm aware of how people tend to view those whose bodies do not function perfectly. It's all bullshit, of course, given that a substantial percentage of the human population lives with some form of illness or disability. But we have been taught in this country that productivity and perfect health are vitally important. Whether it's company wellness programs that lean hard on physical fitness, or our twisted and dangerous diet culture, there isn't much room for people to move through this society with bodies that deviate from an ideal. That's true even though so many of us, in fact maybe most of us, don't conform to what is considered normal.

My own dependency on other people's blood plasma plays into all of this in different ways. Although I spend a lot of money on insurance copays, and probably could have bought an entire house with the out-of-pocket costs I've had over the years, I am but one part of the equation that makes a few companies an awful lot of money. There's a knowledge that has stuck with me in years of using other people's blood to maintain a somewhat normal life: from that scene in Paris memorialized in that oil painting, to the blood transfer experiments in London, to today's plasma sellers in America offering up their arms in exchange for supplementary income and a deep scar, the world of blood is built on the bodies of the poor, giving it to the better-off and making a few select people wealthy in the process. The blood game is rigged, and always has been.

CHAPTER 6
The Vampires of Capitalism

I'm a fountain of blood
In the shape of a girl
—Björk

By the time I began looking into the world of blood extraction and sales, the system had already been strange for a long time. The big players, mega-pharmaceutical giants based around the world that buy and sell most of the plasma that the United States uses to make medicines and conduct research for citizens here and in other countries, have mechanized and sanitized the process, reducing it to an efficient, albeit bizarre, science. People who need money pour into extraction centers around the country to sell their blood parts, and the plasma pours out while the profits flow. It is a gigantic, well-run global machine controlled by a handful of companies that operate across multiple international borders.

America is the primary source of the world's blood plasma, the place with an abundant, available pool of donors in need of extra cash. It is also a place of light regulation, making it a perfect field for extracting the fluid in exchange for a nominal fee. The buyers draw in plasma sellers, then sell the extracted goods or make them into expensive drugs sold through specialty pharmacies in a tightly run, sanitary chain that keeps the risk of viral infection and other dangerous events to a minimum. The odds of catching a virus these days from a plasma donation or a plasma infusion are slim to none in the United States or Europe. I barely worry about it.

Around the edges of this big blood trade, away from the plasma

collection centers, the stories often get stranger and much less predictable. That's where the less scrupulous players in the world of
moving blood emerge, looking for ways to experiment with the
blood and its parts as an elixir and deploying debunked science
in ways that make rational people cringe. There are many stories
about blood as a magic potion and they usually end in a resounding
thud.

California's Silicon Valley of the 2000s and 2010s became
the global epicenter of rich people searching for the fountain of
youth. But this latest immortality fixation on young blood for old
bodies began not with experiments on humans but, as with most
new technologies that scientists eventually want to introduce into
humans, with mice. In 2008, researchers at Stanford University
opened a series of Frankenstein-esque lab trials that sounded at
once like science fiction and a throwback to the earliest, darkest
days of blood experimentation. They wanted to find out whether
the blood of young mice would reverse the aging process in older
mice. It was a theory born of a centuries-old, deadly chronicle of
superstition and magical thinking, one that had been repeatedly
tried before and failed. This time, however, the Stanford experiments not only didn't kill the mice but also seemed to reverse
some of the markers of aging. Things seemed like they might be
different this time.

This is the abusive, ethically fraught experimental history into
which Stanford ventured with fresh ideas when a scientist named
Saul Villeda decided to put myth into practice in mice. The experiments were bizarre, almost grotesque, as he inflicted harm upon
mice in the name of medical advancement. Rather than simply infuse the blood of young mice into old mice, Villeda's team stitched
the animals' arteries together in pairs. In an older process created
to study the immune system, called parabiosis, the scientists joined
the circulatory systems of young mice to those of older mice. The
permanently paired twosomes would then share each other's blood.
These parabiotic tests had been done before, across a span of 150
years in several countries. The practice seems to have been abandoned after a series of failures in New York in the 1970s, when too
many laboratory rats died from a mysterious illness without showing any positive results. The animals in the California experiments,

apart from being sewn together, presented a far more promising picture.

Within a few years, the team started publishing its results in a series of scientific papers that sparked a flurry of headlines around the world. The older mice sewn to younger ones showed reversals of cell damage, a hallmark of the aging process. More important, the changes were found in brain and muscle tissue, the places where aging is most detrimental. That is, as we age, our brain cells and muscle tissue degenerate and shrink, which leads to a host of failures in the system. There is a long road from stitched-together pairs of mice to young blood as a treatment for aging human bodies, but the dreams of eternal youth and unlimited profit began almost immediately. Could it be that the key to human youthfulness was so simple that it lay in the most fundamental of places—the blood of youth itself?

This is not simply an exercise in vanity, though ego and narcissism push much of the modern research. Science is always seeking ways for humans to live better, not just for more years. Human beings are living longer than ever before, the world's overall population is aging, and all these older humans face a cascade of health and brain failures that make us more expensive to keep alive. That can turn what are meant to be the golden years into a far less pleasant experience. By 2034, the United States will have more people over the retirement age of 65 than it will have children under the age of 18. In 2050, the world will have 2 billion people over the age of 60, nearly twice the number it has today. By 2060, the average age in America will rise from today's 38 years old to 43 years old. The story is the same all around the developed world. Faced with these facts, if the key to living better, longer, is simply an infusion of young blood from a willing donor, why not get pumping?

"Do I think that giving young blood could have an effect on a human? I'm thinking more and more that it might," Villeda, the lead scientist in the Stanford mice experiments, told the *Guardian* in 2012. "I did not, for sure, three years ago."

In light of the long history of hope placed in young blood as a youth elixir, it was probably only a matter of time before a few wealthy Americans saw Villeda's mouse studies, conducted at Silicon Valley's favorite university, and took the idea to the next illogical level. As more cautionary science appeared alongside those studies, particularly with screaming warnings that the experiment might harm those hapless mouse twosomes, the enthusiasm dimmed a bit.

A First Mover

Big cautions do not survive long in the world of Silicon Valley, where wealth seeks the fountain of youth and endless vitality. By 2016, Jesse Karmazin, a young medical school graduate with an opaque past, was trying to take this latest fountain of youth concept to the open market. Karmazin's career—which includes an agreement that he will never practice medicine in at least one state because of an undisclosed transgression—was shaped by a hunt for the ultimate cure. He was not part of the Stanford lab trials, but he knew all about them.

It is difficult to know where Karmazin got his inspiration. When I talked with Karmazin myself and asked where he got the idea, he did not mention transfusions as a spark. Yes, he had watched them, but that wasn't what made him move in this direction. The real origin could be the overwhelming hype the mouse studies received, as it was impossible for a medical-adjacent person at Stanford, where Karmazin studied, to miss the high-pitched buzz that accompanied the mouse experiments.

Karmazin, then a slightly chubby man in his mid-thirties with dark hair and a receding hairline, spoke with the hurried pace but practiced neutral tones and slight stutter that were so prevalent in the tech world. If you looked for him on his company's website, you'd see a video of Karmazin dressed in black jeans and a pale button-down shirt, giving a six-minute talk to the Superhuman Summit in Vancouver in 2018. This was an event at which the founders of futuristic companies, their potential investors, and a smattering of self-styled health gurus came together to talk about wild ideas and crazy concepts in "hacking" the experience that is living in a human body.

Even the titles given to conference speakers indicated this event was for an audience living in a rarified environment, one far removed from poverty and living on subsistence-level wages. Past speakers at Superhuman included a "sonic healer," a "self-care innovator," a "genetic steward," and a "sleep whisperer." This was a gathering place for people who wanted to spend their money on improving the physical experience of being alive, and who wanted to make life last longer—maybe even forever.

Karmazin's talk was promoted on the website under the headline "Paradisiacal Plasma." His path in hawking this unproven magic had been less than heavenly. He was not a particularly dynamic speaker, but Karmazin's pitch pulled you in simply by the bizarre nature of what he was offering. We are all aging, little by little, he told the crowd in his opening lines. This is a problem that can be fixed. He led them through a brief history of mice being stitched together to share blood, including one unverifiable anecdote involving a gray-haired mouse who regained its black hair in a parabiosis study. Then he moved quickly into his pitch for taking the youthful transfusions to humans, bringing to life an idea that has been toyed with—and tried without much success—for centuries of human history.

"Our idea is to use, essentially, excess blood from blood banks to help you restore your levels of these growth factors. And this is what it looks like," he said, touching the clicker in his hand to reveal on the screen behind him a photo of his middle-aged parents lying in beds with infusions tubes connected to their arms. "These are my parents, and, uh, they like the treatment. My dad said he felt very energetic . . . ; my mother thought her skin improved," he continued with a nervous smile. "Apparently, it feels really good. People say they feel energetic. . . . We're also seeing a lot of medical improvements as part of our clinical trials."

"I know this sounds like vampires," he said, then riffed a bit about Countess Elizabeth Bathory, the alleged serial killer, bathing in young blood. Karmazin described what he said was the impact of young blood infusions on physical appearance, even his own, as "kind of dramatic." Wrinkles fade, skin color improves, markers for potential roots of disease reverse, he claimed.

And yet, with all these promises, the photo and anecdote about his parents were as close to scientific evidence as Karmazin offered. Though he claimed to have infused the blood plasma of young people into more than 100 people over the age of 35, he would not release any scientific studies on their age markers or general health. He told me the studies are considered intellectual property, and he was not ready to give those details to the public.

What he gave to the American public, for a moment, was an

expensive opportunity to take part in an experiment that's been widely warned against and dismissed by credible scientists. When he founded his company in 2016, Karmazin deliberately chose the name Ambrosia, a Greek word meaning "food of the gods." He saw his notion as nothing less than turning back the clock for human beings. In what he called "self-funded clinical trials"—experiments paid for by the subjects—patients over 35 years old could pay for infusions of verified, pure, and safe young-blood plasma to witness the results themselves.

His pitch was at first irresistible to journalists, not because anyone appeared to buy it, but because the shock value of the idea of moving around young blood to cure aging was too delicious to pass up. Amid a growing landscape of wealth inequality that America hadn't seen in generations, these tales of a real-life vampire operating among the obscenely wealthy tech giants of Silicon Valley seem too on-brand to be true. When Karmazin dropped a hint to one reporter that tech titan Peter Thiel, a founder of PayPal and Palantir and an early Facebook investor, was interested in his company, the excitement boiled over. Thiel is widely reviled in the media world for killing the media critique website *Gawker*, and a tale of him using his extreme wealth to feed on young blood was almost too perfect. In 2017, the television show *Silicon Valley* parodied the situation with an episode called "Blood Boy," in which a wealthy programmer hires a "transfusion associate"—a young man whose sole function is to supply him with young blood.

Empty Promises

There was a problem, however, in that there was no real evidence Thiel was ever interested in Ambrosia. Karmazin later said he misspoke about Thiel, and only Thiel knows for sure. In the early days amid the hype, Ambrosia began offering infusions in Silicon Valley for $8,000 a pop. Young blood, he said, was ethically sourced from donors, the "leftover" plasma that hospitals routinely threw away because they had no use for it.

By early 2019, Karmazin was ready to roll out his young-blood program to the rest of America. Ambrosia selected eight cities around the country, mostly midsized metropolises like Omaha and Austin, where clients could pay from \$8,000 to \$12,000 for each infusion of young-blood plasma. It was, he believed, the natural extension of science and a way to offer this anti-aging remedy to affluent people living outside of Silicon Valley. Karmazin wouldn't say how he chose the cities or how many patients, if any, he had in each, but within a few weeks of opening the clinics, the U.S. Food and Drug Administration stepped in to alert people of serious risks.

"The Food and Drug Administration (FDA) is advising consumers to be cautious about establishments offering infusions of plasma obtained from young human donors with the claim that the infused plasma will treat a variety of conditions ranging from normal aging to memory loss," it warned. "Establishments located in several different states are currently offering infusions of plasma, which were obtained from young donors, to individuals at a cost of up to thousands of dollars per infusion for a variety of conditions. There is no proven clinical benefit of the infusion of plasma from young donors in the prevention of conditions such as aging or memory loss, or for the treatment of such conditions as dementia, Parkinson's disease, multiple sclerosis, Alzheimer's disease, heart disease, or post-traumatic stress disorder. The dosing of these infusions, which can involve large administered volumes, is also not guided by evidence from adequate and well controlled trials."

The agency cited possible infectious, allergic, respiratory, and cardiovascular risks, as well as potential lung injuries, circulatory system overload, and serious allergic reactions. The treatments could be anything but innocuous.

Karmazin told me that the FDA warning concerned him and he wanted more detail. In the weeks after, he tried to get an answer from the agency about what he needed to do to comply with their safety demands, but no answer was forthcoming. When nothing more materialized, he again started tiptoeing around how to bring young blood to aging consumers. The answer seemed to be in scaling back by using a private list of patients, in a single location rather than blanketing the country with infusion clinics. Though he might not have come up with the idea of young blood being the fountain of youth, and he didn't have any current investors in Ambrosia, he was nothing if not passionate about the treatment. "I sort of feel like the purpose of medicine is to make people live longer and healthier," he explained.

———

Karmazin got a lot of attention, but he was not alone in this quest. He was an outlier, a rogue who attempted to use bad science on live humans. More recently, though, a plethora of companies with strange names and big-money backers have begun studying the components of young blood, from stem cells to more specific parts, as potential treatments for age-related maladies. All have staked major investments on big possibilities, but to date Karmazin's is the only one to have offered such blunt proof of concept. And while he got his blood from blood banks, others have drawn some of their research materials from the giant pool of human plasma that is collected across America, for $25 or $30 a pop. The pool is massive, but the demand is even greater. Hundreds of thousands of donors offer their veins each day, and yet there still isn't enough blood plasma to go around. Not only that, but even established drugs—the old ones like mine that work so well—are in perpetual shortage. Between the lifesaving uses of plasma and the futuristic, unproven experiments on how it might be used, there is little middle ground. We don't have enough blood to go around to feed the growing demand by wealthy Americans to live longer, better lives.

CHAPTER 7
Vanity and Blood

Move back from the trench and turn aside your blade
so I may drink the blood, and prophesy truth to you.
—Ulysses, in Homer's *Odyssey*

Blood boys and promises of perpetual youth are a step too far for me, and for most people, but there are much more moderate ways to dabble in the quest for agelessness through blood. For a glimpse behind the curtain, and maybe a little bit out of boredom, I booked a "vampire facial." In all honesty, it was the second year of the pandemic, I was exhausted, and I was beginning to look it. Maybe a fancy blood-infused facial would revive my skin and give me the added bonus of some special insight into the strange things people try with blood as they hunt for the keys to unlock endless youth and vigor. The closest I got were the needles.

In a vampire facial, a technician draws blood from your vein, uses a centrifuge to spin out the plasma, and then, with microneedles, pushes bits of the plasma fluid back into the outer layers of the skin on your face. The use of plasma in the process is the gimmick. Microneedling has been shown to improve the skin's texture and stimulate cell growth. Injecting your own plasma back into the outer layer of your own skin hasn't been proven to do anything at all. I winced at the notion of extraction, of the idea of needles moving in and out of my face, a tiny sewing machine of anti-aging punctures.

It's a practice made famous by celebrities like Kim Kardashian, wealthy women searching for every available means to look younger, better, healthier. It is, from what I can tell, mostly a gimmick. We believe blood returns us to our youth, so adding a dollop of blood to an established cosmetic procedure like microneedling ups the price and the allure. Afterward, the client's face is raw and red for a few days, but there is much debate over whether anyone looks younger. Maybe a little pinker. Still, it was a lesson in the appeal of these practices. I had fleetingly thought it might turn back the clock. There is almost no science to back it up.

Bloodthirst threads through our oldest stories: the use of others' blood, often those younger, more beautiful, riper with desirable qualities, to sate our own desires. Homer's *Odyssey* is rife with blood, the hero Ulysses drinking the blood of two sheep he has killed to give him the power to communicate with the spirits of the dead:

> Then the ghost of Theban Teiresias appeared, carrying his golden staff, and he knew me, and spoke: "Odysseus man of many resources, scion of Zeus, son of Laertes, how now, luckless man? Why have you left the sunlight, to view the dead in this joyless place? Move back from the trench and turn aside your blade so I may drink the blood, and prophesy truth to you."

When I read these stories, it occurs to me that I'm one of the small fraction of people on the planet who does benefit from regular, large quantities of other people's blood. Without the plasma extraction centers and legions of blood sellers spread from Flint, Michigan, to El Paso, Texas, to Rexburg, Idaho, I would lose my ability to work, to thrive, to live. Vampire facials make for dramatic Instagram posts, a Kardashian's gorgeous visage oozing in tiny, perfect droplets and smears of her own blood. It's as though her beauty comes at great personal cost, not by virtue of being extremely wealthy. But they aren't health; they aren't real life. Experiments like Ambrosia hinge on shoddy science and the misplaced hopes of the uber-wealthy— just another version of what's always been.

It seems that, for many people, blood represents something that might save them or make them feel better, more vital, more alive; only a few of us actually do live this way, in a perpetual cycle of need, not merely desire, for other people's blood. As I write this sentence, I'm sitting in an infusion chair with a plastic IV tube stuck in the crook of my right arm. It connects to a tube hooked into a clear IV bag that's filled with yellowish fluid. The particles of thousands of other people's plasma, through which I can look out the window for a distorted view of the mountains, will drop into my vein for five hours on this day. My hands and feet are intermittently numb at first, but I know that within twenty-four hours the liquid made from other people's plasma will stop whatever attack my own immune system has mounted and I will begin to feel normal again.

In the few weeks between my last infusion and this one, in 2022, Sony Pictures released the latest Hollywood take on vampires, a bomb but one I found quite relatable. *Morbius*, a story from the Spider-Man comic universe, is the tale of Dr. Michael Morbius, a wealthy doctor who has spent much of his life searching for a cure for his own rare blood disease. In the beginning, the actor Jared Leto plays Morbius with an exaggerated limp, pale gray skin, and the outlook of a sickly genius. Morbius finds his cure in the DNA of vampire bats, which leads him to become a living vampire, lush with youth, vitality, and good looks. The dark side, of course, is the doctor preying on human victims to feed his need for blood.

The "Summer of *Morbius*"—a publicity promise that morphed into a social media joke—never materialized (the film flopped with critics and audiences alike), but that's not usually the case with vampire flicks. From the unofficial Dracula adaptation *Nosferatu* way back in 1922, to *Interview with a Vampire* in the 1990s, to the *Twilight* series of more recent years, the vampire genre has provided rich fodder for filmmakers. Audiences . . . drink it up. There's something about the vampire story we just love. What's better than the tale of a person mending their ills with other people's blood, then transforming into a creepy creature in the dark of the night? Jared Leto's limping along on crutches and his sickly pallor read as dreary nonsense to many, but I found his ridiculous character entirely too relatable—minus all the murder and immense wealth tied up in the plot.

Part of me wishes the reality of depending on other people's blood was even just a little bit as glamorous as any vampire flick. Vampire lore is an entire subset of American pop culture. Blood as an elixir, a youth tonic, a cure for anything, is too hard to resist as a storytelling device. We love the idea that other people's life essence can reverse the damages of illness, time, and wear on our own bodies. But here, in my hard, red, fake-leather reclining chair at the infusion center, the whining drone of a pump pushing fluid into my vein humming in the background, I can tell you that modern medicine's closest approximation of vampirism is quite tedious.

I try to read but taking a Benadryl beforehand to fend off potential allergic reactions puts me into a daze. Each time, it is monotonous, and I am bored, vaguely entertained by hour after hour of *Law & Order* on the infusion room's television. By the end of the day I start losing track of plot details and the time. When I return to the infusion room again in a few weeks, the same episodes might play again, in the exact same order, but I won't even notice that I've seen them before. This is not exciting, dramatic, or age reversing. It is unpleasant, messy, expensive. I don't feel or look younger, but I am alive, maybe even thriving, because of other people's blood.

I went looking for more, this time in what many call the birthplace of the American middle class.

CHAPTER 8
Hollowed Out and Never Enough

Here I am, having to sell
a part of myself to be able to do this.
—A plasma seller in Michigan

If there's a single state where you can trace the story of the United States' industrial rise and decline, and along with it the collapse of our fragile social safety net and what people do to get by without it, it might just be Michigan. I have always been allergic to the phrase *real America* or anything resembling it. You can't find the story of the entire country in one diner in the heartland. I don't believe in the notion that any one state or city encapsulates what has happened in this country in the twentieth century and beyond—but still, an awful lot of that story can be found in Michigan. On my map of plasma extraction centers, this state is marked with red dots where the plasma centers cluster in areas of economic decline. The Rust Belt is full of these places, and they are almost always busy with people selling their blood protein.

Knowing this, I flew east to explore blood selling in Michigan cities that felt familiar to my own former Rocky Mountain boomtown, albeit bigger and far more racially diverse. To Detroit, the grand city whose spectacular collapse, along with the auto industry it was built around, and promising rebirth has been chronicled at great length; and from there I drove to Flint, where the locals still don't drink the water, even though its famous poisoning catastrophe has been pronounced solved. In these old industrial hubs, once the beating hearts of American labor and industrial creation, selling plasma has, for many, become a stopgap to make up for lost job security, absent pensions, low wages, and scarce government help.

In a lot of cases, the people I found selling plasma were not those whom I expected. That felt true in all the places I visited, though. I had assumed I would find mostly the unhoused, the unemployed, the people who simply cannot make money any other way; they would be selling their plasma on the margins. But the reality of plasma sellers is more complex and says so much more about how our country is devolving into ever-widening economic disparity. The paid-plasma industry has deliberately "regulated out" the most vulnerable members of society and instead relies on people who work in precarious jobs and low-paying industries. A little driving tour around parts of Michigan gave me a peek into the place.

Live from Michigan

Lansing, Michigan's capital, has about 112,000 residents now, down by nearly 20,000 people, with a steady loss of population since the 1980s, when the auto industry that had sustained it began to wither. In recent years, the city has become a hub for resettled international refugees, giving it new vibrancy. It's both a college town, with East Lansing home to Michigan State University, and a working-class community. The auto industry remains Lansing's largest employer, with more than 4,200 workers. The city felt busy, buzzing, interesting, with some broken remnants of the industrial landmarks of the Rust Belt.

While driving around town to look for its plasma centers, I stopped off to get lunch at a Burmese restaurant. It was tiny, set back in a gritty old strip mall off a busy street, but it was owned by a family from Myanmar and the food was authentic and great. In that one moment, I could see this was a place built upon a whole lot more nuance and depth than those silly, pervasive clichés about the white working class.

In Lansing, as with most of the rest of the region, it felt to me like the plasma business was booming, subsidizing incomes for college students and workers. It was one more stop on my quest to find out who's selling their blood, and what I found in Michigan was a little bit of everything.

A woman I'll call Melissa moved to the Upper Midwest to start what would be her second job as a journalist in local TV news. She grew up in a small rural town a few states away, where her family and most of the people she knew held tight to conservative political views. When she went off to college, she was drawn to a group of a young people who leaned politically more left than the folks in her hometown, and that appealed to her. Politics had become even more divided during those years, and she wanted to find a way to lead people to common ground. For Melissa, building a career in journalism seemed a natural way to bridge the two increasingly polarized spaces, digging up stories and information to connect diverse communities, and inform both her friends and family members of tangible facts rather than feed partisan political fodder.

Her first journalism job after college was as a reporter at a small television station in the West, where she covered the spectrum of stories. The pay, as it tends to be for most people working in local television news, wasn't great. Still, she loved the work and, more than that, she believed in the mission of local journalism. After two and a half years in that job, Melissa moved up in the world of television news and found a better, bigger position farther east.

When we spoke, Melissa told me her salary was not a whole lot more than what she had made in her first job, but the cost of rent was much higher in her new home. She was cautioned by colleagues that she should live in a pricier part of town, for safety reasons. Moving to an unfamiliar city can be challenging. Paying her rent, basic living expenses, and often shelling out for her own gas to drive to story assignments around the state added up. Right after she arrived in her new home, Melissa began thinking about a college friend who had sold her blood plasma to pay the bills. It seemed so easy for that friend, she thought, and it was a way to contribute to society by giving a lifesaving substance to critically ill people. Why wouldn't everyone do it to make a little extra money? That's how it began for Melissa.

Back when she worked in her first television job, there were no plasma extraction centers nearby, when she first entertained the idea of selling her plasma. That city was likely both too small and too wealthy, quickly becoming a resort enclave for the uber-rich, a beacon for second-home owners and monied vacationers. Plasma centers tend to cling to cities on the decline, where real estate is cheap, or at least to places where a lot of people who need money are nearby.

I first met Melissa through Twitter, where over the course of several months I also found dozens of other people who sell their plasma to get by financially. Social media can be the next best thing to standing outside an extraction center, in terms of meeting donors. She was excited to talk about the process and how it has helped her keep on top of her living expenses as she builds a career, one she hopes will lead someday to international reporting. We chatted over Zoom, where she explained how plasma selling works for her.

Melissa was in her late twenties, with sunshiny good looks that made her a perfect fit for television. She was a good reporter, a naturally curious person who knew how to weave together the details in a way that made sense. Because we're so conditioned to think that people who sell their blood plasma are only the most marginalized members of society, it might surprise her viewers to know that, twice a week, usually after a full day of work, this young, smartly dressed professional whom people see when they turn on the nightly news drove across town to have her vein tapped so she could buy groceries and other necessities. She was not the person most of us would expect to find selling plasma, but she was also not all that unusual for what she has had to do to make money. What I was beginning to learn was there was no stereotypical person who sells plasma; the common thread was that of going through a rough patch in personal finances.

In the beginning, Melissa said, the idea that she needed to sell a piece of her body to get by in life simply made her sad. That was after college, after all, when she was working full-time in her chosen field. She had reached a point where her career was beginning to take off, yet she still did not have enough money for the basics of a decent, maybe even fun, life. It felt surreal that she was working in a high-profile field she'd studied to join but was still not quite able to get by without something else. Even without having student loans to pay off (her parents helped cover the costs for school), a local TV news salary simply did not cut it. *Here I am, having to sell a part of myself to be able to do this,* she thought. Melissa got past that part pretty fast, however, and she integrated the plasma center visits into her life. It was part of her schedule, as much as going to work and to the gym and anything else.

————

After Melissa and I spoke, I thought back on my own beginnings in journalism. At this point in my career, twenty-five years down the road and making a decent living, I might be tempted to wonder why anyone would enter a field that forces them to sell their blood for groceries. I don't wonder, however, because I was in that same spot long before selling blood was a possibility. I've also met too many younger colleagues who have sold their plasma at one time or another when they couldn't find any other way to make their finances work.

My first real reporting job was during a summer while in college when I spent time covering the city and county governments for the local newspaper in Missoula, Montana. I was paid a total of $700 at the end of three months for what accidentally morphed into a full-time job. It was supposed to have been an unpaid internship involving a few hours of work a week, but the parameters changed when one of the newspaper's staff journalists walked off the job and the editors asked me to step in. I jumped at the opportunity without thinking about the pay, which seems ludicrous now. To cover my rent and bills while reporting full-time for what amounted to free, I worked another full-time job in a busy downtown Asian fusion restaurant. A typical day that summer meant conducting interviews with local government leaders and city residents in the morning, breaking for a few hours to work a shift on the lunch rush at the restaurant, then going back to the newsroom to write the story. At night, I either went back to the restaurant or to city council meetings. I didn't do much else but work.

It was a lot to handle, and I was exhausted and broke all the time, living in a shitty rental space with a roommate and not having much fun outside of the endless work. I was also 20 years old and somehow thought that was how it was supposed to be. It was still possible to work for minimum wage and pay the bills then. Truth was, I loved it. I had internalized the idea that, if you work extra hard, a thriving career will reward you in the end.

The peculiarity of this belief only hit me one day that summer when I interviewed the mayor in the morning about a new city budget, then served him lunch in the restaurant a few hours later. He was a head-in-the-clouds type who didn't notice that the newspaper reporter he'd talked to in the morning was the same person taking his lunch order. The mayor's blank-faced response as I waited on him in the restaurant makes me think about the scientific studies that prove most wealthy people don't actually "see" those who are of lower economic stature. The city manager, who was with us in both places, had recognized me right away. He's still a friend all these years later, but the confused, maybe a bit embarrassed look on his face when he realized I had two jobs shook me out of thinking this was a normal way to live—working one tough job for low pay and another one for almost nothing. I did it anyway, because at the time—the mid-1990s—we were taught that climbing up the ladder into a middle-class job in news was still possible. Those years were the tail end of that career path being viable for most people in the industry.

Years later, I realized that a select group of people who start with the most help in terms of money and connections do earn substantial salaries in the national media, but that's rarely true of local or regional news. Having worked in both, I know there's little discernible difference in terms of skill; the divide lies primarily in resources and staffing. Larger companies hire more reporters and editors; they have bigger budgets. Generations of institutions presenting the occupation through the lens of a calling, rather than a career, has led thousands of young journalists, most of them working in local news, into situations where media companies exploit their labor; that's just the way it is. Unless you are born in the right place, have enough money and wherewithal to get into an expensive private college, or have the connections that allow a foot in the industry's door by starting in national news, journalism is not a well-paid profession and hasn't been for a long time.

When I started, I thought I was doing the work of the people, speaking truth to power, exposing corruption, and digging up details that otherwise would remain unknown to my family, friends, and neighbors. I did manage to do all those things, but too often at the cost of great stress and little reward. I still believe in the mission and importance of reporting work, but when I look back, it's obvious that by subsidizing my journalism career with restaurant work and other gigs, I was padding the bottom line for a series of companies that made huge profits through sales and advertising, and by paying their core employees low salaries. For young journalists starting out now, especially in nonunionized newsrooms and covering cities, towns, and state governments, the landscape is sparse. I can't imagine that I'd choose journalism as a career if I were starting out today.

A Withering Industry

Since 2008, the number of people employed in American newsrooms has fallen by 26 percent from 114,000 workers, according to studies done by the Pew Research Center. Smaller newspapers have been hardest hit in the gutting of local news, losing more than 50 percent of their total staff in that same period of barely over a decade. While national newspapers like the *New York Times* and *Washington Post* have grown, made more money, and expanded their staffing in recent years, the power in the news business has become increasingly concentrated in a few major cities like New York and Washington, D.C. The newsroom where I worked at that first reporting job in Missoula is long gone, the building sold to developers who are planning luxury condos in place of what was once the heart of the community. This same story repeats itself, time and time again, across the country, in towns where once-thriving spaces of information are replaced with national stories that fail to bind the community, or even inform it, often polarizing people in their politics.

In Penny Muse Abernathy's ongoing study of which parts of America are suffering the most through the decline of local news, the former professor at the University of North Carolina Hussman School of Journalism and Media points out what she calls "news deserts"—places that no longer have a local newspaper nor access to one. The deserts are widening and expanding, like the Dust Bowl, and in their place are voids of critical information with no solid source to tell people what's happening in their neighborhoods, cities, and states. Abernathy's research has revealed that more than 200 counties across the United States have no local newspaper, and in many other communities, like the city where I live, the remaining newspaper is a ghost of its former self, hanging on with few staff and sparse reporting of the stories people need and want. This absence of information was even more evident during the pandemic, when our shrinking local newspaper printed little more than basic, sometimes outdated information from the local health department and a few details about who was sick or dying. The result was a perception of distance from the virus, a sense that what was happening might not be a real threat.

Studies have also shown that when local news shrinks, people tune in to the national conversation. The details of community life get sketchy, the realities of everyday experience are murky and untold to those who don't live them. Donald Trump was like entertainment, a horrifying circus act, especially in contrast to the bland stories that fill the local newspapers in many places. When people don't have good, engaging information about what's going on in their own cities and towns, and instead they focus on the national news, they become more politically polarized, hardened in their partisan identities, and less willing to consider—and possibly vote for—competing political candidates. The pandemic, as it has done with so many of our systems already flawed and under severe strain, accelerated layoffs and closures throughout the industry. In other words, local news is dying at a time when we need it the most. With the collapse of local news, stories like the ones I turned up in reporting this book, the small-scale crises that contribute to broader trends, fade into the background.

By several accounts from people who work in local television news, Melissa's corner of the industry has fared a little bit better than local or regional newspapers, but not by much. The pay is stagnant and seemingly endless staffing cuts mean that journalists are often one-person crews expected to operate their own cameras, interview people, report the news, and produce their segments. Melissa often had to fund her own travel expenses for work. All that technical work—jobs once done by news teams—is now handled by one lone person who has to work smarter and harder than ever before to find the stories and tell them well.

The Vanishing Road

When I left local news in the early 2000s, I was earning $37,000 a year at a job covering state politics and government in Montana, and even that wasn't a great salary. Almost twenty years later, Melissa, who was doing close to the same job with more demands, in a bigger state for a larger audience, on television, made about $44,000. When she told me how much she earned, it all began to make sense. If I'd had the option of selling plasma instead of restaurant work way back when I did that first newspaper job, I would have jumped at the prospect in a heartbeat.

Back in my hometown, a local journalist told me she'd like to start selling her plasma to boost her income, but the town is too small for a donation center and the nearest one is more than an hour's drive away. The money from selling plasma would be eaten up quickly by the cost of gas to get there. She would look for a better-paying job or consider selling her plasma when she moved to a city that had an extraction center. I winced, hearing this part of her economic plan for the future—it's not just a temporary fix for a short-term struggle.

Working in local news often requires people to get creative about making extra money. I freelanced for a while for a national outlet when I got more established, but I had a boss who allowed me to do that. The largest boots-on-the-ground endeavor is Report for America, which bills itself as a national service program that sends emerging journalists out into the working world and subsidizes their salaries at local news organizations. For years, I worked for a global news start-up also created by one of the group's founders, so I've seen its progress along the way. On the good side, Report for America sends hundreds of journalists into places where news might otherwise go uncovered. On the flip side, those journalists often move to places they don't know or have ties to, and they don't seem to stick around. The pay might be okay, but I've spoken with several "corps members," as the organization calls its young journalists, who would like to subsidize their earnings with extra work; local news wages are too low. They can't, however, because Report for America's contract bans them from taking second jobs to prevent conflicts of interest, and instead requires them to do community service projects. Maybe that's where selling plasma comes in.

———

That's how Kelsey, which is not her real name, ended up selling her blood plasma. As a Report for America corps member based in the

Midwest, she needed extra money when a friend asked her to be a bridesmaid in her wedding, to be held in another city. Travel, the special dress, and other costs associated with the wedding added up quickly. Selling her plasma seemed like the best and only solution. None of her friends were shocked. "A lot of my friends are local journalists, and we all do weird things for money," she told me, laughing.

Kelsey signed up to sell her plasma at the Biolife center in the city where she lived, and she found a special offer whereby new donors could earn $800 for six donations—a "huge amount of money," in her words. That offer made the difference between scraping by and being able to enjoy her friend's wedding, as well as having some extra money. The problem began with her first donation, which left her so drained of energy, she found the experience frightening. On the days she sold her plasma, she had a hard time doing much of anything else. It was a lot of money and it would pay for what she'd long planned, but the physical toll sucked. "I'm a pretty active person. I would be wiped out for the rest of the day and all the next. If I tried to exercise, I just could not," she explained.

She had sold her plasma about twenty times in the last couple of years, saving up money from one series of donations to pay for applications to graduate schools. But Kelsey had to cut back on her trips to the plasma center because the fatigue she felt after having her cells extracted made it too difficult to carry on with her normal life. She began to use the plasma sales as an emergency funding source, where she could rely on the money occasionally but not use it as a steady source of income.

Kelsey grew up in Michigan, where she knew a lot of people who were broke and selling plasma was common. Even so, disclosure did not come easy. She had not told her parents she was doing it for extra cash, because she didn't want them to worry about her. She did not believe the practice crossed any ethical lines, but her family might have thought she was in desperate straits if they knew about it. This is a story I heard often from younger people who sold plasma. They did not feel it should be stigmatized, because it's just one more way to make money. As the industry has expanded, it has become a more widely accepted way for people to increase their incomes. Kelsey even wondered if it wouldn't be better to remove the money component from plasma donation altogether, since the stigma keeps it grounded in a segment of society where it's become a necessity rather than a gift to others.

———

Melissa did not experience the same kind of fatigue that Kelsey and some others who sell plasma described. She was used to it, going to the center two days of nearly every week for almost a year. There was one time when a needle technician missed the stick, leaving her with deep bruises on both arms that disqualified her from donating for several weeks. They paid her for that day, but she was not allowed to go back until the bruising had cleared up. I asked what she did for necessities in those weeks, and the answer was bleak. She went through her clothes and sold items online for extra cash, but it still was not enough. "I bought fewer groceries and ate less," she said.

Melissa at first didn't tell her family about her method for earning extra money because she didn't want them to worry. She was, after all, not marginally employed; it should have been enough for her salary to cover all her living expenses. She had all the marks of a young person moving ahead in their chosen profession, one that could bring her to great places. There was a tell, though—the deep scar in the crook of Melissa's elbow. She worried that people who see the scar might think she's a drug user. I heard this fear expressed repeatedly from others, even though the plasma scar is unique. A person injecting drugs would not use a needle so big; the scars would be smaller and more scattered, as they would be searching for fresh spots on the veins. In the world of plasma extraction, the inner arm divot marks the spot of extraction, not injection, so it's the site where so many Americans feed a deep demand for human plasma.

I had a long conversation with Melissa about what would be fairer for plasma donors like herself. In a society where millions of people need extra cash and others need the plasma to treat their illnesses, should we leave the costs and rewards up to the free market? People like me depend on other people's plasma to live a normal life and, in some cases, to stay alive. I could see the surprise on Melissa's face when I told her how much my medication costs—$12,000 a dose—although that amount changes all the time with weird market fluctuations. The disparity between that amount and the $800 a month she was paid to donate twice a week is a yawning chasm of disparity. Obviously, a lot happens between the extraction center where she gave and the infusion center where I get. Plus, the medication I use is made from a plasma pool containing hundreds or thousands of donations.

Even given those caveats, I think the gap between buying and selling prices remains too great. I told her about Luke Shaefer, at the University of Michigan, and his proposal to develop a plasma donor minimum wage—an idea that seems like basic common sense. Shaefer's notion is that rather than companies constantly shifting their pricing schemes and offering incentives targeted at bringing people back as often as possible, for months and years on end, they pay donors a fair minimum rate each time they sell their plasma. Melissa's eyes widened as she thought about the possibilities of a guaranteed fair price for plasma.

"Did he tell you what the minimum wage should be?" she asked. He did not give me a specific number. But the payment for plasma needs to reflect a person's time and the potential toll of the protein removal on their body. Right now, profit-making companies control each aspect of the endeavor, from setting the prices to encouraging donors to come back repeatedly. They don't pay for labor but rather offer a pittance for time. Even though the financial reward is ultimately payment for blood, it's couched as something else. It is labor, to my mind, like any other form of work, and yet the effort is not compensated in a transparent or established fair way. The people who sell their plasma are not told how the prices are set, where they are set, or by whom.

CHAPTER 9
The Rust in Our Veins

*They left looking a bit more tired, marked like wounded soldiers
with a brightly colored single loop of elastic bandage encircling their arms.*

A few miles west of downtown Flint, past the hulking dingy white fortress of Flint Assembly, Vehicle City's last remaining big factory, the Mill Creek mall sat languishing under Michigan's flat gray winter skies. Like so much of the sprawling industrial city of Flint, a place built around an industry that has mostly abandoned it, the mall was built for much more than what remains today. More people, more businesses, more cars, and bigger, better times.

The guts of the retail shops that remained within the stucco shopping center were scarce when I showed up in late 2021, but one section of the rutted parking lot was filled with dozens of cars from before dawn until late in the evening. Sandwiched between a struggling discount furniture store and Ollie's Bargain Outlet, the CSL Plasma donation center drew a steady stream of people nearly every hour of every day.

They pulled up in the parking lot in beater cars with busted windows and in brand-new pickup trucks. They were dropped off at the door by family members who came back an hour later to pick them up, or they walked across the parking lot from a city bus stop. They left looking a bit more tired, marked like wounded soldiers with the brightly colored single loop of elastic bandage encircling their arms just above the elbow, holding pressure on the spot to prevent bleeding where the needle had entered. Their ongoing parade, in one door of the center and then out another an hour or two later, represented a cross section of Flint's population: Black, white, young, middle-aged, some limping, some strutting and joking with the friend who had joined them for company and maybe to make a few extra bucks themselves. They were all here for the same reason: to earn some money and to serve some abstract greater good by lying back in a chair for forty to sixty minutes while a medical technician and some whirring machinery mined their bodies and blood for liquid gold. It was hot—too hot to stay in the car—when I took up my little stakeout position in the parking lot and waited for people to leave the clinic so I could talk with them. I had learned it's easier to grab people on the way out, as when they first arrived they were in a hurry to get in the door and get the process moving.

This center was one of the five paid extraction clinics within striking distance of downtown Flint. That's one paid-plasma center for roughly every 16,000 people, as much a marker of the city's economic decline as is its notorious toxic water scandal and its pockmarked highways, both the result of an entire infrastructure built for a city that was once more than double its current size. By comparison, Missoula, Montana, a much wealthier town that has roughly the same population as today's Flint, also has a large college campus—a favorite target of the plasma brokers—but only one paid-plasma center. It's an industry that marks in bricks and mortar the rise and fall of wealth and struggle across America, often concentrated in communities on the economic ropes, and setting up shop where people are financially unstable enough to sell their blood for gas, groceries, and money to go to the movies. Flint is perhaps the most glaring example I've seen of the disintegration of the middle of America's working class, and how vampirism has swooped in to feed on the remains.

Inside the front door of the CSL Plasma center was a reminder of the mission's greater good. Facing a row of cushioned chairs, a poster showcased this location's adopted patient. It was a marketing gimmick, one that reminded me of the 1980s TV charity campaigns that featured pictures of starving children in far-off lands as incentive to give money to mega-nonprofits. I laughed and thought, *Hey, that could be me on that poster.* The donors and the company were providing a service that benefited me, but they were also making profits in the process. In the poster hanging above the waiting area was a pair of disembodied, outstretched hands that held a picture of a young boy who needed a medication made from sellers' blood, the visual evidence that this practice was for a greater good. I found myself wondering if the donors would want to see me—a middle-aged white woman who's been using their plasma for years—on a poster. I'm not quite as sympathetic looking, I thought, as a sad child.

But the truth was, the people in line barely glanced at the boy in the poster. They were not there to perform an act purely of charity; they were there to earn some money. Many were regulars, I found from talking with folks, people who came in twice a week to have their veins tapped and to collect the maximum amount of money. At that time, the max was $1,100 a month, depending on coupons and promotions. If you didn't get sick or miss your ride. If you weren't too tired from working your full-time job. If the tech didn't miss the needle stick and blow out your vein, putting you on a deferral list for weeks or longer. It was a steady, small income dependent on good fortune in many ways, and good fortune isn't what people selling their plasma in Flint have amassed a lot of in recent years.

Industry analysts and academics have studied the presence of paid-plasma donation centers across the country, and their locations tell a clear story of the country's economic conditions. Across the Rust Belt, in former industrial strongholds fallen on hard times in Michigan, Ohio, and nearby states, where metropolitan populations remain relatively high but residents earn less money and have diminished access to good jobs, the plasma centers spring up. In the Southwest, these clinics line the Texas and Arizona borders with Mexico, drawing another country into the cross-border blood trade. The plasma economy leaves a mark on nearly every state in the union, but it prefers those with larger populations.

While the Rust Belt is riddled with plasma extraction centers, there were some blank spots on my map of the industry. As one researcher told me, the reason for their smaller numbers on the Upper East Coast is likely due in part to higher wages. Some regions have no paid plasma centers at all. And then there's Flint, a small city that's weathered decades of hardship heaped upon it by corporations and corruption. In the 1970s, Flint had 200,000 people, but today its population hovers around just 80,000. The five paid-plasma centers placed strategically in stand-alone buildings and malls around town were rarely short of people waiting to roll up a sleeve and stick out their veins.

It's in Flint, once the heart of the American auto industry and the city that lays claim to creating the modern middle class, where I finally get to see the inner workings of the plasma extraction business. On a wide, rutted highway that stretches south of the city, I drove past the Little Darlings strip club, some gas stations, and a peppering of fast-food chain restaurants. I was looking for the familiar outline of one of the country's largest plasma extraction brands. The building stood out on this run-down section of road, a newer freestanding facility between businesses that have seen bigger, better days. It was a cookie-cutter design that looked like a nice medical clinic sitting among the older, shabbier establishments on the highway.

I showed up at this specific plasma center for a job interview, but I didn't actually want the job. I'm entirely unqualified to work in a plasma extraction center. I have no medical training and my hands are unsteady, but I wanted to see the inner workings of the operation.

At the Source

A friend of a friend of a friend arranged a meeting for me, because the only way I was going to see how the industry works on the inside was by talking to someone about getting a job extracting other people's blood. Since I was there slightly undercover, the only solution was to roll with it and pretend to be looking for employment. I put on my best job interview face, a big smile, and commenced asking as many questions as possible of each staff person I met. The center is owned by one of the three major plasma extraction companies that operate all over America. Its management team was looking for new workers in the middle of a killer pandemic. In other words, they were a little desperate. Extracting personal fluids in a setting filled with hundreds of people was not the kind of job most people wanted.

The plasma clinic's waiting room was modern and tidy, lined with neat rows of chairs and cheery signs about saving lives. It was a warm, clean space for donors to wait their turn to be processed via the computer system and then escorted back to the donation room. One of the managers told me this place extracted about 1,200 plasma donations in a typical week. He estimated that about half of those weekly donations came from regulars, the folks who showed up two times a week to earn the highest dollar payout possible. It was a stunning hint at the volume of this local plasma economy. The other half of the donations were from new plasma sellers who came in on an irregular basis, looking for quick cash. A few who came in were experimenting with the practice to see if the payoff was worth the effort. The raw number of people in this one extraction clinic shocked me. I did a quick bit of math while waiting to be taken into the back for a tour, based on the fact that Flint has roughly 80,000 residents. If each plasma center in Flint got a similar number of donors each week, that equated to 6,000 plasma extractions weekly—one for each person in what amounts to nearly 7.5 percent of Flint's population.

This was a city burdened for decades by the devastating departure of a major industry, left in poverty and hard luck; as a result, many of its people were oozing plasma in service of pharma industry profits so they could make ends meet. The sheer volume of donors made it clear the plasma industry was both supporting and depending on a significant number of residents in an economically distressed community. Flint's population is majority Black, and because Black Americans statistically earn less than their white counterparts, this also means the industry is preying on people of color more often than on white people. This appears to be a pattern across the Rust Belt, in the South, and in the Southwest along the border with Mexico.

Inside the Flint paid-plasma center, at the counter, I made small talk with the assistant manager while we waited for the director of the center, who had to run out on an errand. In the meantime, he gave me a tour of the operations so I could get a feel for how the place worked. In all this, he never asked me how qualified I was to work there. It felt like I had stepped into a television comedy skit, but I nodded along and asked questions at every stop on the tour of the guts of this plasma center. I wondered if he could tell I wasn't actually there for a job. I put on my best poker face and moved through the facility like a woman on the hunt for work. I nodded along as he pointed out different parts of the center and introduced me to staff along the way. I asked as many questions as I could, which he seemed to appreciate. There's a trick you learn when you work as a journalist for long enough, which is that people love being asked about themselves, their work, the mundane details of their lives. Here, it helped to conceal my actual purpose in the place.

We stepped behind the front counter, where he waved toward a team of technicians who were running through the health screenings with a few prospective donors. One potential new donor sat with his arm stretched out across the counter, the sleeve of his blue shirt rolled up, while a tech took his blood pressure. Another potential donor answered a routine list of health questions to check if he was eligible to give plasma, a process that's repeated every time a donor returns. In the beginning, there is a finger stick to draw some blood to test for viruses and other issues. If this is a donor's first time, they will be paid for the time, but the plasma is not used until the second donation. The blood is screened for hemoglobin and protein levels—a key to ensuring the health of the person losing their fluids.

Then we walked into the back, where a wide room opened up to reveal tidy rows of dozens of recliner chairs. About twenty people were lying back in the chairs on this day, their veins already tapped and attached to long tails of tubing that wound into a machine— one machine for each person. The machine extracted their whole blood, spun out the plasma, and returned the red blood cells to their body through the same tube threaded into their vein. There was a moment, looking around the room, when I felt woozy, like I might faint. It passed quickly, though, without any notice from the assistant manager. He didn't seem to catch my reactions at all.

At first glance, the extraction room might look like a center where cancer patients and others like me get their infusions. But it's too big, there are too many chairs, and if you watch closely, the little whirring machines next to each chair are different from infusion pumps. They are self-contained blood mining and processing centers, and there is one per person so as to avoid cross-contamination.

I watched as a short, young Black woman began the process of giving up her blood to the waiting centrifuge by the side of her chair. She looked slightly uncomfortable, maybe just not happy to be there, shaking her left leg with anxiety. I let my eyes wander across the room and noticed two other men, already attached to the extraction machinery, also shaking their legs. It was chilly in the room and having the blood removed, spun through metal, and then reinjected cold into the body can make people even chillier. Several donors brought their own blankets from home.

The young woman about to be stuck had her navy blue winter puff coat stretched across her lap for warmth. A phlebotomist in a mask and medical scrubs moved toward the inner crook of her elbow with a 17-gauge needle. As someone who has had dozens of infusions and needle sticks, I knew what it meant when my guide mentioned the size. The needle is exponentially larger than the 22-gauge one used to infuse medication into my veins. A larger needle makes it easier to slide a tiny tube into the juicy, fat vein that sits inside the elbow. It is also more painful than the tiny barbs used on my hands; knowing this, I cringed at the idea of a sharp spike going into the woman's arm. The larger circumference of the plasma needle, and the wider plastic sheathing left inside the vein when the needle is withdrawn, also allows for an easier draw of blood and the return of red blood cells to the donor.

It was in this moment when I needed to turn away and stop watching. Even after all these years, I still have needle phobia and I feel a physical revulsion when I think about the prick of skin and tissue that allows the plastic tubing to slide into a vein. In truth, it doesn't hurt much. It's more of a pinch, but knowing what was going on made my chest flutter. As I saw the needle hovering above her arm, it brought back to me the dozens of missed IV sticks, when my own nerves or a nurse's poor training left me with bruised and blown veins. The assistant manager, a jovial man of about 40, told me this was the hardest part of the job, but you got used to it after a while. I thought to myself, *Nope, there's no chance I'll get used to it, and, honestly, I'd faint if I ever worked here.* But I smiled and continued nodding as he talked.

Some plasma center techs miss and blow a hole through rather than pierce a donor's vein, especially in the beginning, when they aren't fully confident about needle insertion. A bad miss can leave the donor unable to give plasma and earn money that day; it's a problem that requires finesse by the staff and a good attitude about customer service. It was during this little break that I realized the job for which I was pretending to interview was a phlebotomy position that included six weeks of on-the-job training. I stifled the urge to shout out to him that, given the shaky state of my hands from years of minor nerve damage and a lingering fear of needles, I could more easily fly than stick another person with a 17-gauge infusion needle. The idea of it, and my circumstances in the back room of this plasma center, seemed hilarious to me, but I needed to keep a straight face. Instead, I resumed asking questions, keeping the conversation moving. The assistant manager didn't seem to care. He hadn't figured out what I was really doing there.

On that day, the center's sleek recliner chairs held maybe a third of the people the room could accommodate. Some watched shows on their phones; a few others played games. One man read a book, and a woman in the next row talked to someone on the phone. Everyone looked more than a little bored. I thought of the tedium of sitting in a similar chair, receiving the drugs made from their plasma, another shared experience. About half the donors were Black, half were white. Flint's population is just over 54 percent Black, so the racial makeup here seemed to align with that of the city. It was the same with the staff.

The big room was quiet but for the buzzing and clicking of the machines and a few muted conversations. The assistant manager told me the place did offer free Wi-Fi, one little perk of donating plasma. There were not many other perks, though I was also told the staff kept a reserve of juice and sugary and salty snacks like cookies and crackers on hand in case someone felt faint when it was all over. They didn't hand them out, however, unless someone truly needed a little pick-me-up.

None of the sellers in the chairs looked especially happy to be there, but they would all get paid. I couldn't ask them questions, as I was on a fake job interview, but I guessed they were mostly resigned to the task at hand. Next to each donor hung a plastic IV bag, hooked up to the tubing that wound in and out of the centrifuge, slowly filling with liquid. This was the plasma, the liquid component of blood: the fluid gold that fuels a multibillion-dollar trade.

When I have my infusions, I do so in a private room at a health-care clinic with my own space and a television I control. I bring my laptop to do work or browse the internet. I talk on the phone. I stare out the window. Sometimes I doze off, but only for a few minutes. I am, in a lot of ways, incredibly lucky to have decent health insurance that covers the treatments in a comfortable place with private rooms and a nurse who rarely misses my vein. Still, I hate it. The whole process takes five or six hours, and it is incredibly boring. Luckily, I need to do it only once every two months or so. I thought about how crabby I would get if someone suggested I get stuck with a needle and sit in the extraction chair in a big room full of other people twice a week. Just the dullness of it, coupled with the coldness of the place and the roomful of strangers—it felt quite sad.

Livestock

When I toured the plasma extraction center in Flint, demand for plasma in the still-lingering world of COVID was high; fewer donors showed up than in previous times when the virus wasn't such a threat. Inside the Flint plasma center, my thoughts returned to the way so many donors have described the process: it's like a dairy, and we are the cows being milked.

I returned my attention to the chatty assistant manager, who still didn't catch that I was not entirely engaged in our conversation. I asked more questions, something about the needle stick technique. We moved on to another step in the process. In a separate room off to the back, several workers prepared and sealed sterile kits that were assembled in advance. Each plastic bag included the IV needle and tubing, the plasma collection bag, and other fresh medical supplies. The kits were stored in neatly organized plastic bins. When plasma sellers were escorted to the common area with the reclining chairs, their tech opened one of the sealed bags, ensuring none of the supplies had been used or contaminated. The process was clean, run like a modern, efficient medical clinic.

This setup was nothing like the grotesque prison-inmate plasma extractions in a big gymnasium in the 1990s in Arkansas (I'll get into that later), or the reused equipment that caused the deadly blood scandals in rural China in that same decade. The place felt clean, efficient, and safe. The physical risk to donors of contracting a virus or other contaminants has been reduced to almost nil through careful steps built on scientific lessons learned over the years about viral transmission and contamination. On my side of the transaction, the risk is equally low.

As we chatted, the assistant manager explained the rules of the system, which included requiring donors to have a physical home address, thereby eliminating the possibility that unhoused people can sell their blood parts for cash. The logic behind cutting out segments of the population was never clearly explained, but I gathered it was related to perceptions about the unhoused and potential drug use. When the full picture emerged, it became clear this wasn't a process aimed at the very poor, but rather one that has been established and maintained as a supplement in a society that lacks full support. I had walked into this investigation thinking I would find the poorest of the poor, but the truth was that group was mostly barred from selling their plasma at all. My own peril in receiving a medication made from plasma is not one of viruses. The drugs I take do come with lists of risks, including blood clots and other frightening possibilities, but my main concern now is the anxiety that arises from thinking about how the medication is produced. I'm not pilfering blood from unhoused people; I'm depending on those who make just enough money to barely make ends meet.

Marginal Payouts

This is a calculated business decision designed to minimize the health risks, balanced with the knowledge that there is a steady stream of people who need just a bit more money.

The business of buying and selling blood plasma began almost as soon as we figured out it was a valuable tool in medicine. Today it's an elixir that people need and pay for. Throughout the 1950s and 1960s in the United States, small collection centers lured in plasma donors, both paid and unpaid. Their plasma cells were mostly used to make medicines to treat hemophilia—a clotting disorder that can kill if it remains untreated. But ever since plasma-derived medications were developed in the 1960s, the demand for whole blood and blood plasma has outweighed the available supplies of both. Donating blood takes time, and for some people it can be painful. A lot of folks are squeamish at the sight and thought of giving up their bodily fluids, including me. There is a segment of the U.S. population that sees it as a duty to give blood, but many more don't like doing it. Selling plasma goes a step beyond that, for most people.

In the beginning, pharma suppliers faced a shortage of blood and plasma donors, but money soon crept into the system, a lure for people who might not otherwise show up. Around the world, there are gruesome stories of the blood trade—some of them still make me shudder, even after all these years of using plasma. I knew well what happened in China when safety fell by the wayside as poor people and profiteers rushed to get rich on blood. But I wanted to know more about blood debacles in other countries and what we might learn from them, and especially how they might relate to America's massive blood-seller brigades.

Blood in the World

There is no shortage of blood-extraction horror stories in recent world history. One in particular, linked to the United States, fed political intrigue into a plasma extraction pipeline whose end point was in this country. In 1978, the assassination of a newspaper owner and editor in Nicaragua exposed a world of shady blood-plasma deals that traced directly back to the country's ruling dictator, Anastasio Somoza Debayle. Critics of the president claimed he was involved in a company that extracted the plasma of poor Nicaraguans and sold it to an American branch of that company at a huge profit. Journalist Pedro Joaquín Chamorro was murdered, in part, because his newspaper had exposed the president's involvement in the plasma collection company. That a military government's leader was involved in the extraction of poor Nicaraguans' blood for export seems so heavy-handed as to be a tall tale, but international reporting bore out the truth of the matter.

Then-president Somoza denied the plasma profiteering charges, but the story lives on, including tales of the twenty-four-hour operations of Managua's "Casa de Vampiros" ("House of Vampires"). Inside that building, the blood plasma of poor Nicaraguans was extracted and sold for use in the United States. The people who gave their blood were paid $5 per time, while the regime is said to have pocketed the remaining money. This was more than two decades before the U.S. plasma economy took root, but also when biomedical companies needed plasma to make the new drug therapies they had begun to develop. The fluid had to come from somewhere, and a poor country run by a dictator willing to export his citizens' blood plasma became one source—for a while. The House of Vampires was burned to the ground in one uprising, and the Somoza government was eventually overthrown, but the weight of the story lingers.

The global drive to create a plasma economy began almost as soon as scientists learned how to separate the golden fluid from red blood cells. In the 1950s and '60s, doctors began treating immuno-compromised patients with injections of immune cells derived from plasma, and it was the creation of infusion drugs made from human immune particles—like the medication I use—that pumped up the industry into what it is today.

In 1973, the U.S. company Cutter Laboratories began clinical trials with immunoglobulin that was infused into a vein, rather than a painful series of injections into muscle. With that development, the industry blew up, but it required a big pool of raw material to do so. The World Health Organization has consistently discouraged the practice of paying donors for blood, so pharmaceutical companies made a work-around for plasma donors—a token payment in the United States designed to compensate donors for their time. Though the language remains couched, the compensation is higher than the U.S. hourly minimum wage, and it has become an essential income source for millions of Americans.

Today, just five countries in the world allow plasma donors to get paid: the United States, Austria, the Czech Republic, Germany, and Hungary. Among them, the United States has by far the largest number of people who need extra cash, with the result that we have a massive industry, with Americans supplying some two-thirds of the world's plasma. This includes a substantial share of the blood plasma used in Europe. The European Council also frowns on the idea of paying people for plasma, so in the end its citizens are often using medications made from American blood, which likely came with a financial payout.

While the physical risks on both sides—of giving and receiving plasma—have been reduced, and, for me as a recipient, explained at length, what lingers is a big question of the physical and mental exploitation of those who sell their plasma. I watched the women in scrubs and masks assemble the sterile kits inside the Flint plasma center, but there was no talk of the personal lives of the donors nearby and what troubles brought them in the door. Some donors told me later they got to know the staff, but it's often a love-hate relationship. Even the ever-changing payment rates and bonuses paid for their bodily fluid are set far away, by the management at a parent corporation on another continent.

The managers of plasma operations get a payment list and promotional rewards assigned to their facilities by a computer-based system, those financials already having been calculated far from the economic and social troubles of U.S. cities like Flint. The game is established and its rules are set beyond our borders, but the system is dependent on our brand of inequity and economic struggle. At the Flint plasma center, I wondered if the assistant manager thought about any of this. Other plasma center employees I've met in the last couple of years know about the unfairness factor of this equation, but they don't spend a whole lot of time dwelling on it.

———

As my tour continued, I grew even more confident I didn't want to work in a plasma extraction center. We strolled into yet another room, a large walk-in freezer kept at constant subzero temperature. It was similar in look and feel to a walk-in freezer that would be used in a restaurant, but here it was kept even colder. It was stacked with sealed plastic bags of human blood plasma instead of meat and produce. When the donors' plasma was extracted, still warm, in its plastic one-liter bags, it was brought immediately to this freezer and flash-frozen. Each bag was tagged with a scannable barcode that connected to the donor's personal chart, stored in the company's database. If anything went wrong with the bagged plasma, the source of the problem was traceable back to the exact time, place, and person.

In the deep-freeze room, solid bags of plasma sat for several days while more were added to the stacks. It reminded me of manufacturing assembly lines I've visited, but here, human bodies supplied the parts. Twice a week, refrigerated trucks showed up at the back door and the drivers filled their cargo space with hundreds of bags of human blood plasma, then rushed them off to the processing plants. From there, the plasma of people from Flint, from Rexburg, from all parts of the country went to laboratories for research, or to health facilities for use directly in some medical procedures, or to pharmaceutical companies' production lines to make medicines for patients and scientists around the world.

This single center in Flint, busy as it was, represented just a tiny starting point of a well-lubricated global supply chain. It all depends on the donors, and on keeping them coming back as often as possible, for as long as they can. The body renews its own plasma supply. The donors who return regularly begin to rely on the money and become like a bottomless oil well, their inner arms tapped repeatedly, needles navigating the nests of scar tissue to find the vein where that precious fluid lives.

As we finished our tour, I walked back with the assistant manager to the front counter, past the rows of recliners and the donors seated alongside their whirring extraction machines. We stopped to chat for a few more minutes and I noticed an unfamiliar odor in the air; I couldn't ignore it. I asked him about it—what is that peculiar smell? In my mind, I knew: it is the overpowering odor of blood. It was also the acrid smell of the chemical injected back into people after they finish their extraction. It might seem strange, but how could a place that mines people's bodies like a rich vein of copper not smell of blood?

Mixed with the blood smell I detected the sweat of anxiety and a strange chemical odor I didn't recognize. The assistant manager said I probably noticed the smell of a common anticoagulant used in the extraction process, a substance that prevents the blood from clotting before it is returned to a person's arm. That drug is routinely used in medicine, but some plasma donors report how this part of the process makes them feel ill and brings on worries about the long-term implications of its use. I wondered what it would be like to work in a room with this smell five days a week. Did you ever get used to it? Did it linger on your clothes when you went home at night? It stuck with me for the rest of the day, so I imagined it was the same for plasma center workers, but more routine.

By that time, the general manager returned from his errand, so he, the assistant manager, and I walked to another room for the official part of this little charade. Across an oval conference room table, I again asked most of the questions, my strategy for getting through this ninety-minute meeting without laughing or running away. What surprised me was they never questioned my qualifications to work in a medical-adjacent field. I have none. What they wanted to know about was my customer service experience. As we talked, I told them about working in restaurants and stores, all true stories, but from a lifetime ago.

During the interview, a picture emerged that keeping the donors content and returning was a priority here. My lack of qualifications did not seem to be a problem so long as I knew how to make the customer—in this case, the person getting paid for their plasma—a little bit happier in the process.

Somehow this makes sense. An industry so exploitative—one that pays just enough to draw people in and keep them coming back, but not enough to provide a living—would need to massage the rough edges to make a palatable practice. You can miss a needle stick here and there, maybe leave a bruise or two, but you can't scare off potential plasma donors with bad customer service. You have to know how to deliver bad news, and sometimes bad luck, with a smile, without making the customers unhappy. It's a real skill. And from what I can tell, there are a fair number of unhappy plasma sellers out there who need to be reassured and calmed down.

It wasn't that different from working in a restaurant, except that I would have been sticking people with a big needle and drawing their blood plasma into a big plastic bag. After thirty-five minutes of asking more questions than I answered, I sensed I was losing my grip on this fake interview, so I told them I had another appointment and needed to wrap this up. The assistant manager asked again for my résumé, and I once again assured him I would send it as soon as I got back to my computer. As the manager walked me out, he told me I could probably have a job as a phlebotomist if I wanted one.

I wondered: *Is it this easy to get onto the first rung of the ladder of an industry that churns human bodies for profit?* Back in college, I had worked an endless rotation of customer service jobs—in restaurants, a clothing store, and a record store. The lingo I used to answer the manager's questions was similar to what I'd say when I worked in retail. Like so many other manifestations of American capitalism, the trick to making the game work is to convince people that their exploitation is a good experience, fun and positive; that their contribution is valuable and that they are being fairly compensated for their time or effort. Plasma extraction companies do this in part by deploying the sorcery of coupons and promo codes, so sellers rack up points in the same manner as in the loyalty programs used by airlines and hotel chains—a lottery of potential bonuses and tiny windfalls instead of a solid, straightforward pay rate for people selling a part of their bodies.

———

It's a puzzle for sellers to work out, and people love to navigate little mazes that end in higher payouts. Americans love to gamble. The payment schedules and promo codes and bonus days trigger people's dopamine release centers, like racking up a good hang on a poker machine. When it feels like a game, it feels like you can win. Plasma sellers can believe they are gaming the system, but they are in a system that is always gaming them. Visiting the Flint plasma extraction center, I learned that customer service is part of that game. The smiling faces and pleasant attitudes conceal the truth of what's going on and who's winning.

CHAPTER 10
Flint

When they smile and say,
"No raise in pay!" Sit down! Sit down!
—Maurice Sugar, song from the 1936–37 GM strike

A hulking white-and-beige industrial ghost, the General Motors Assembly Plant on Van Slyke Road in Flint takes up the space of a small town or large neighborhood. It covers several city blocks and has room for thousands upon thousands of laborers to make cars. These days, only a small fraction of the massive factory is still running. Van Slyke Road is one of the many highways in Flint that feel a bit too big for a city that's lost half its population since its heyday. Today's Flint auto plant, which still employs just a little over 5,000 workers, is a tiny fragment of what this city used to be in the juggernaut of the American auto industry.

The looming physical presence of the GM campus was once just one among several auto plants in Flint. Now it's the only one that remains standing. The rest of the city's auto plants have been torn down, plowed under, and, like much of the city, left to live in people's memories and in history books. There are historical markers all over downtown, and photos of old, bustling Flint on the walls of cafés, and the archway over the city's main street that still reads "Vehicle City." The nickname dates back to the city's buggy-making days in the 1800s and it has stuck and survived through today.

I drove around the city and its sprawling highways, marveling at how a place built for double the number of people has diminished and been left to fend mostly for itself. Pockets of hope seemed to spring up from the ruins in the form of small shops and community events; there were signs that Vehicle City might be on the path to a comeback. But it was impossible to forget how the auto industry had its way with Flint, and then all but abandoned it.

Across the road from the old auto plant lies the headquarters of the United Auto Workers' regional offices, one of a smattering of union offices still scattered around the town. I was not here for the union office itself but to explore the monument that had been constructed in its backyard. It was easy to find, though overgrown with weeds and littered with trash. Captured in sculptures that fill the small park is a scene from the Flint Sit-Down Strike of 1936–37. Men in work clothes sit in an imagined auto factory, unmoving, on car seats in the outlines of an auto plant. Some men read newspapers, while others sit chatting or looking off into space. Along the edge of the sculpture's factory outlines, a group of women come to support the striking men. One is approaching the strike with a picnic basket; another swings a billy club above her head, getting ready to smash through the glass. A third woman is being dragged away by police or company goons—I couldn't tell which.

This scene, re-created in life-sized bronzes behind the union office, captures a moment when police and company agents tried to disrupt the strikers' supply lines and force the men back to work. The men sitting inside the plant don't seem to notice what's happening to the women, presumably their wives and relatives. They are focused on their task: occupying the factory by simply sitting down and refusing to work. The scene is both quiet and violent, a rendering of a unique labor strike tactic that brought the automobile industry to a halt for weeks and changed the way workers were treated in Flint, and beyond. When the company refused to improve working conditions, the auto workers simply sat down in place, in chairs and on the floor, and refused to work or to leave the factory. Management tried to argue that the striking workers should be arrested for trespassing, but the strike wore on.

The Flint Sit-Down Strike, at the time a novel method of demanding better treatment from a massive company, united a fragmented group of auto workers' unions formed only a couple of years earlier and lasted forty-four days. In the end, it drew concessions from the company for better wages and factory working conditions for the men who worked in the plant. It happened fast, but by all accounts the company pressed its workers too hard and they dug in. President Franklin D. Roosevelt urged the auto company to recognize the union and accept its demands, and ultimately the industry emerged stronger, in large part because of its workers. The gains won in Flint inspired workers around the country to press for better working conditions and higher wages in a series of major wins for organized labor in that era, which helped create stronger, wealthier communities with a functioning social safety net.

How It Used to Be

In oral histories preserved from some of the sit-down strikers in Flint, several men who worked in the plant described why they took part in such a dramatic and potentially dangerous action to demand better from the company. They told of how conditions inside the plant were bleak, that managers were demanding backbreaking work with no respite and little concern for their well-being. Their descriptions bring to mind the worst aspects of America's industrial revolution and are sadly resonant of the situation for many workers today. "You couldn't get a drink of water," plant employee Joseph Martinus told an interviewer. "You couldn't even go to the bathroom. What I mean is, you was tied down that closely."

This history feels not so different from the wrenching labor practices of contemporary American life at companies like Amazon nearly a century later. Back in the 1930s, it was enough to drive the families of Flint to dramatic action. I grew up in a union town—Butte, Montana—where copper miners in the 1910s and '20s organized unions in the face of corporate and state violence. Flint's story of union growth and busting, the boom and contraction of work, of mass production and organized labor, feels familiar—those waves of work I've seen in my own lifetime, but centered around mining for valuable minerals. The players are different, the patterns are the same. Each labor movement in America has its own singular history, but they coalesce around the fact that direct action by labor can create better conditions for workers and their families; that sharing the wealth that is produced rather than corporate hoarding of profits makes for better, stronger, more vibrant communities across the country.

If you spend any time talking with journalists and historians who live in and know Flint, it does not take long to hear what they see as one of the most important contributions to this city's history. With this kind of direct action and a large, racially diverse workforce, Flint created the blueprint for the American middle class. Life in this city for a few generations back then allowed working people to work hard in tough jobs and rewarded them well, thanks to the momentum of organized labor. Some historians fear it was a short-lived phenomenon, falling apart in later years as American economic disparity grew. Following the big strike and into later generations, auto companies in Flint provided decent jobs, good benefits, and a reliable path to earn a fair living without a college education. Flint was a place of abundant family housing, tight-knit communities and close social lives, hard work, and often good fun. At its peak in the '70s, Flint had nearly 200,000 residents. Their lives and the city's economy were structured around the auto industry, where General Motors employed 80,000 people in Flint alone.

In the late 1980s and early '90s, GM began to gut its U.S. production lines, shutting down plants and laying off thousands of workers. By 1989, when documentary filmmaker Michael Moore chronicled the decimation of his hometown in the film *Roger & Me*, GM had reduced its Flint workforce to 50,000 people. In the film, Moore intersperses chasing GM CEO Roger Moore around the country for an interview with devastating scenes of the lives of those who remain in Flint. Many families left the city, while those who could stay faced unemployment, mass evictions, and the taking root of what would become generations of poverty.

The homes and grand buildings were emptied, their bones left to decay. One in every six Flint homes was abandoned as families fled to other parts of the state or country for work and safety. In the remains of this industrial abandonment is a staggering poverty rate. Almost 40 percent of Flint's residents live beneath the federal poverty level. In this era, it has become a city ripe for the picking by the blood extraction industry. The median household income here—the place locals will tell you birthed the middle class—now ranks in the bottom twenty cities in America.

Flint's population and its power are greatly diminished. But in my three visits to the city, stretching over the span of nearly a year, I found many reasons for optimism in the place and its people. The residents believe in the future of Flint; they want to build it into a better version of what was left behind by the auto industry. The city has cleaned up many of its blighted and abandoned buildings. The former local newspaper office is a thriving downtown farmers' market; community shops and bookstores have sprung up in re-imagined spaces of grand old buildings. There is a buzz downtown. Flint is reinventing itself in spite of all the problems that have been dumped on it, first by corporations and then by corrupt government officials.

The auto industry still stands, but it is a skeleton of its former self. Today, GM employs about 5,300 salaried workers in Flint, mostly in the large white plant near the strike memorial, where they assemble large Chevy and GM trucks and family SUVs. The industry, with its legions of workers who built the American middle class, is a shadow of what it once was. In its wake, so many have left, and those who remain are working to create a new Flint.

Feeding the Beast

I found the Flint Sit-Down Strike memorial by chance. I had driven to this part of Flint, on the outskirts, to look for a plasma center, one of the half dozen red dots across this city that are plotted out on my map of the American blood extraction industry. Flint's wide, often empty roads can be tricky to navigate, and I ended up on the wrong side of the highway. The cluster of sculptures caught my eye, so I stopped to check them out. I was a little lost, but the place I had come looking for was also right there, within walking distance of the strike memorial. Across Van Slyke Road, near the remains of the auto plant, Talecris Plasma Resources had set up shop in a brick building that was busy day and night.

Each time I visited Michigan, that plasma extraction center and its parking lot were full, its lobby brimming with blood sellers. You can't see the strike memorial from that parking lot, but it's right across the road. In a place where jobs were once good and plentiful, the plasma business has swooped down to prey upon the remains. A plasma center in sight of one of the bedrocks of American working-class labor, where there is little but a memorial wrought from metal about its history to tell people what this place means. Sometimes the metaphors employed to describe cutthroat American capitalism, racism, and classism are just too heavy and obvious to make any sense at all. I was struck by the moment, the weeds growing up around the sculptures commemorating the strike, in contrast to the tidy, sparse landscaping of the plasma center. Organized labor centered on the work of making cars is the old Flint, and probably the old America. Modern America is about doing whatever it takes to get by, and that might mean selling a piece of your body.

It was in the parking lot of the plasma center, looking across the street at the old auto plant, where I met Randy, a 41-year-old Black man whose father worked for GM when his family was young. He did not want me to use his real name, because a lot of people in his family didn't know he sold his plasma. He didn't want to make them worry. He didn't want to have to explain it to them.

Randy was dressed in jeans and a gray sweatshirt, and he flashed a bright smile when I approached him as he walked out of the building toward his car. Once again, a lot of people seemed to think I was trying to sell them something when I asked to talk with them outside of plasma extraction centers, but Randy was friendly and chatty. He told me his dad retired from GM, but by the time Randy was old enough to work at the factory, the great contraction of American car manufacturing was well underway and there was no space left for him.

It once was the case in Flint that a job at an auto plant was a given for guys after they graduated from high school, but those days are long gone. So Randy worked a series of retail and restaurant jobs until he decided to take training courses in IT. Tuition ate up a lot of money, and by the time he finished, he was married and had a couple of kids. He now had a job maintaining the computer systems for a local company, but the salary was not enough to raise his family as comfortably as his parents could when his dad worked at the plant and his mom had a part-time job.

When we spoke, inflation had pushed up the cost of food and gas beyond the wages Randy earned, and his family already lived on a tight budget. Twice a week for the last few months, he had come here to sell his plasma and make extra cash to bridge the gap. It's what he'd done off and on over the years for extra money that usually went toward gas and groceries and the occasional night out for dinner with his wife. He was, like most people who sell plasma, just used to it. Randy described how Flint had changed and said he never would have guessed as a kid growing up here that he'd be selling his blood to make ends meet. It's easy, he said, but the time and hassle are a little annoying. The whole undertaking should pay more.

As we spoke in the shadow of the GM assembly plant, I asked Randy if he had the telltale plasma donor's scar. He pulled aside the elastic bandage around the crook of his elbow and showed me the dark mark there. It is, he said, just what you have to put up with to get the money. It's annoying, but it's not a big deal. He did have some concern that people might think he'd been using drugs, even though the scar was all wrong in placement and type. Plasma sellers know the difference, but they worry about what others might think.

Then Randy paused, leaned in a bit, and told me plasma sellers really ought to be paid more. He could make up to $1,200 a month if he showed up twice a week and signed up for all the promotions and coupons. The needles did not bother him; the worst part was the boredom. Randy watched videos on his phone and caught up with friends by text messaging, but it was a grind to sit in the extraction chair. For him, selling plasma ate up at least three hours at a time, between driving to the center, checking in, and the hour it took to draw cells, then wrap his arm in elastic and send him home. I told him that my latest medical bill showed a dose of human immuno-globulin, possibly made in part from his blood, cost my insurance company more than $12,000. He burst into laughter again. We both did. The disparity is absurd. There's no other way to see it.

———

Randy was one of about a dozen people I talked with in Flint as they finished selling plasma. Across town, in a different extraction center in a run-down strip mall, I found other friendly people willing to talk about blood selling. The residents of Flint seemed a bit more concerned about the stigma of plasma selling than those I had met back in Rexburg. In Michigan, folks were a little more reluctant to talk to me or to elaborate on why they did it. But once I explained myself, plenty of them opened up with their stories. They were, like almost all the others I've interviewed around the country, doing it mostly for the money.

In conversations with plasma sellers across Flint, when I told people I might have gotten some of their plasma through my medication, they showed a mix of reactions. Some seemed happy to have been able to help; others seemed to suspect I might be making it up. Everyone was a bit caught off guard. I can only imagine that it's weird to have a stranger approach you in a parking lot to ask a series of personal questions about something you don't often discuss, then drop a line about how you might have helped make her life better. But I did it anyway, as it made my own work feel a tiny bit less predatory.

One woman told me she hated giving up plasma and would stop as soon as she found a better job. Another saw it as a quiet way to spend a few hours a week away from her two toddlers—her husband took care of the kids while she sat in the extraction chair. Both of them worked outside the home, and her extra income helped pay for part-time child care.

A white man in his fifties told me he was using his plasma pool to save up for a family vacation to Florida the following year, putting every penny of the blood money aside for plane tickets and hotel rooms. A younger Black man said he didn't separate out where he spent his plasma money. The dollars that accumulated on his prepaid debit card, refilled each time his plasma was removed, went toward the same expenses as the hourly wages he earned at his regular job. The plasma money was just icing on the cake. In the weeks he sold his plasma, he was able to go out with friends more often and felt more at ease about his finances. He preferred to show up at the center in the late afternoon to prepare for the full day's exhaustion he was left with afterward. By the time he finished, it would be getting dark and he could just head home, have dinner, and go right to bed.

The Costs of Selling Plasma

Outside the Talecris Plasma extraction center, the donors I met talked a lot about food. It seems to be a preoccupation of many people who do this regularly. A low protein level on a blood screening can put a donor on the deferment list, unable to sell again for a few weeks. Randy outlined for me his pre-donation meal: in the morning it was three fried eggs, bacon, two pieces of toast, and a big glass of milk. And water. So much water. Dehydration is the enemy of easy needle sticks and can make the whole process more painful and slower.

Dehydration is something I'm well acquainted with on the receiving end of the chain. The day before each of my infusions, I drink five liters of water, an enormous amount for one day, but it helps. Becoming a human water balloon makes my veins stand out and the entire infusion flows faster and easier. Water also cuts back on the killer headaches that can hit me after an infusion and, I think, eases the chemical burden on my kidneys. I drink even more water as the infusion goes on. Over the years, I've learned that these little techniques might be psychological, not rooted in biology, but they help as much as taking anti-inflammatories and an antihistamine before an infusion to ward off potential allergic reactions.

Nutrition is a major part of staying healthy while selling your plasma, but I do wonder how much of a donor's money goes back into keeping up those nutrition levels. Plasma sellers are told to eat healthy, but eating well is expensive. After they left the building, their arms wrapped in tight, brightly colored elastic bandages to stop the bleeding, a lot of donors said they were tired and hungry. Several told me they would drive or walk straight to the burger joint or a convenience store like Khirfan's Blue Collar Market, across from the old auto plant, to stock up on salty, rich snacks. I also know this feeling from being on the other side. Stuck in an infusion chair for five to six hours, my preferences lean toward a can of Pringles. I don't know why, but the richness of comfort food and junk food helps while my veins are filled with particles made from others' blood.

We were talking about the small pleasure of junk food when Randy made another point. He told me that the plasma donation process would be a lot more humane if the centers gave their donors some snacks and drinks during the process. It would, of course, cost them some money to put chips or fruit out for people, but it would make the process a little better for those who fill the plasma bags and cold storage rooms. The way it's structured now, Randy guessed that probably 5 percent of the money he made from selling his plasma went right back to the special diet he needed beforehand and the snacks afterward to feel right.

A few bucks here and a few bucks there, along with gas money to get to and from the center, added up and ate away at the money on his plasma prepaid card. In thinking about the nutrition aspect, I find it hard not to make brutal comparisons through the looking glass of the plasma economy. Human beings treated as livestock, kept alive and fed just barely well enough to ensure the blood flow is coming. People who sell their blood plasma need nutritious, rich food to keep up their health and strength to make the practice pay enough to be worthwhile. This was one of the key components of the plasma study conducted by Xi Chen in China. Xi, the scientist in charge, speculated that Americans would fare better than their Chinese peers in selling plasma frequently because they have access to better foods. But that's not the case for many Americans. The industry's success, at least as measured in the number of clinics and their humming busyness, seems an insult on top of the decades of injury Flint has already suffered.

In each of the three times I visited Flint, I heard the same refrain from well-meaning family and friends at home in Montana. I laughed it off, but it's the stigma attached to a city that's been kicked many times while it was down. "Don't drink the water." This was true even in 2022, although the crisis began nearly a decade earlier, after elected officials changed the city's water supply from treated water from Detroit to a system of drawing water from the Flint River. The river itself wasn't the problem. Running the untreated water supply through old lead pipes fouled the water, leaving many of Flint's children poisoned by the lead.

The city's tap water has been declared safe and drinkable, but questions remain for a lot of people, and many locals still didn't trust the water supply. Elected officials broke their trust with the people with bad decisions and cover-ups, and the cracked social contract is nowhere near restored. Flint's water crisis, which left this majority Black city poisoned for years, was created by corporate and government malfeasance and neglect. The city's water scandal remains the event most people know about this city. Even the downtown hotel where I stayed still handed out bottled water at check-in.

In the era of the water disaster, Flint's population declined further still. For so many poisoned by lead in their water, it hadn't been safe. People in Flint seemed tired of talking about the pipes and lead-laced water, especially with outsiders like me. It barely came up in conversation, and it's a difficult subject to broach in a litany of other hardships inflicted upon the city and its people.

In the course of this investigation, someone asked me if I was worried about getting lead poisoning from my medication, given all the blood plasma extracted in Flint. It's a strange question, but I can see why they asked. The water scandal became synonymous with the city, baked into its identity. The plasma extraction industry is partly clustered in this place that's been poisoned. But there's no science behind the idea that lead from Flint's water would show up in my drugs—it's not a real concern. Instead, what bothers me is the exploitation of people who have already lived through decades of tumult.

I come from a place left behind, like Flint. An old mining town, once a company town created by an extractive industry—copper mining—and then left to wither, so I get Flint and its current state of affairs in many ways. It is familiar in its character and in the way outsiders tell jokes about it. But the town where I come from is largely white, and it is close enough to new development and tourism money to qualify as booming these days. It is also too small to draw in the plasma extraction centers, at least so far. It's not lost on me that the ongoing jokes about Flint's water are made at the expense of the people left behind, with no choice. Generations of Flint citizens' blood was poisoned by lead in their water. Biomedical companies now mine that same blood, churning through thousands of Flint's arms each week, for its proteins.

CHAPTER 11
The Father of Blood Banking

As you know, there is no scientific basis for the separation
of the bloods of different races except on the basis
of the individual blood types or groups.
—Charles Drew

The U.S. plasma economy was first developed upon a series of life-saving advances in medicine, innovations created by people who probably wouldn't have foreseen their science turned into a strange, significant slice of the American export economy. Modern blood history is littered with wild tales of taking chances against strong odds, many of them while scientists were seeking ways to save the lives of soldiers wounded at war.

There is probably no story more intriguing than that of Dr. Charles Drew, a Black man born in Washington, D.C., in 1904. Drew was a gifted athlete who went to college in Massachusetts on a football and track scholarship but who was drawn to biology while working with a favorite professor who saw his potential. The study and practice of medicine was deeply segregated then; there weren't many opportunities in the United States for a Black man to train and work as a doctor. Though Drew died in 1950, several biographers have retraced his life, and historian Spencie Love has disproved the myth that surrounded his death—one that had been easy to believe given America's long history of racism.

After getting his degree in biology, Drew moved to Canada to study medicine at the prestigious McGill University, according to several accounts of his early life. He was the first African American person to earn a doctorate in medicine at Columbia University in New York City, and he went on to work as a head of surgery at Howard University in Washington, D.C. In the 1930s, he began researching new techniques for separating plasma from blood and for collecting, storing, and banking blood in ways that would eventually lead him to direct a massive wartime blood collection effort in Great Britain during World War II. That he did all of this in a racially segregated field is remarkable.

As the wartime head of the U.K.'s Blood for Britain project, Drew developed methods of getting badly needed blood supplies to soldiers fighting on the front lines. Drew developed new techniques that allowed plasma to be spun out of the blood and stored for later use, then figured out the logistics of getting plasma supplies shipped to where they were needed. His breakthroughs led to the modern technique of blood banking, whereby blood and plasma can be extracted from donors, stored safely, and used at a later time for patients in critical need. The medical staff no longer required immediate donors or blood on hand for patients, as the lifesaving plasma was collected and preserved for later use. Drew's research led to countless offshoots of modern medical techniques that have improved and lengthened millions of lives away from the battlefield, including my own.

Drew's life and career were marked and shaped by the racism and segregation that defined America. Racist policies influenced where he lived, where he studied and worked, what he was allowed to research, and which patients he could treat. And yet, Drew pioneered a technique that revolutionized modern medicine. In 1941, he created the first American Red Cross blood bank; yet as a Black man he was not allowed to donate his own blood to that program. A year later the policy changed, but the blood remained segregated. It's one piece in a long line of discriminatory blood practices that extend to this day; for instance, most gay men are not allowed to give blood or plasma, owing to the stigma attached to HIV infections, even though techniques have been developed to screen for and kill any virus in the blood from all donors.

In his time, Drew fought the systematic discrimination against the blood of Black Americans. He drew political heat for his scathing critiques of the Red Cross's anti-Black blood policy, but he refused to back down. In an interview recorded for NPR's Story Corps series, his daughter Charlene Drew Jarvis recalled her father's unwavering stance on the matter. Her father, she said, knew there was no scientific basis for excluding Black Americans from donating blood. She continued: "Further than that, he said, 'You need the blood. We are at war.'" Eventually, his common sense and science won out over the extreme racism of the system. In 1942, the Red Cross changed its policy and Black Americans were allowed to give blood to the banks Drew had established.

The story of Charles Drew's battle against discrimination while making some of the greatest biomedical breakthroughs of the twentieth century became so well known over the years that an urban legend arose. Whitney Young, executive director of the National Urban League, wrote the following for the *Amsterdam News* in 1964:

> It happened one April day while he and three other doctors were driving to attend a medical conference at a southern university. Near Burlington, N.C., their automobile swerved to avoid an object in the road. Drew was critically injured and began to lose blood rapidly.
>
> His colleagues flagged down a passing car and rushed him to the nearest hospital. At the door, he was turned away. It was a "whites-only" institution. By the time he was taken to a nearby "colored hospital," Dr. Charles Drew, the man who developed the theory of blood plasma and pioneered the blood bank, had bled to death.

The story is not true, but it is entirely believable, given the persistent discrimination against Black Americans in medicine. The myth's long and lingering life does reveal a deeper truth about our society. Drew lost his life as he drove to a medical conference in Tuskegee, Alabama, with three other doctors in 1950. He fell asleep at the wheel, his car crashed, and he was killed. But the story isn't so neatly told after that. In researching her biography of Dr. Drew, *One Blood*, North Carolina historian Cornelia Spencer "Spencie" Love found that Drew had not been turned away from a hospital after his accident. (It actually mirrors an incident that happened months later.) "The Drew legend is not literally true, but reveals a larger truth at the heart of Black culture," Love wrote. "It demonstrates the continuing psychological trauma of segregation and racism in American life."

Dr. Drew was only 45 when he died, but his legacy remains large. "He is referred to as the father of blood banking, but during the Second World War, the Red Cross denied the right of African Americans to give blood, which meant that Dr. Drew couldn't himself have been a donor," Drew's daughter said of him. "I think Dr. Drew would call himself a determined teacher and surgeon. And if that took taking a stand, that's what he did."

CHAPTER 12
Crime, Punishment, and Plasma

I would sell my kidney if I could have,
in order to pay for probation.
—Emily, plasma seller in Texas

Blood and criminal justice have a tangled history in America. While the plasma extraction business screens out the unhoused and most of the poorest Americans, the people caught up in the justice system are another matter.

Emily lives in Midlothian, Texas, a small town twenty-five miles outside of Dallas that functions mostly as a suburb of the oil metropolis. With three cement plants and some 30,000 residents, Midlothian is often referred to as the cement capital of Texas. It's even better known as the hometown of Chris Kyle, the Navy SEAL who served multiple tours in Iraq and was immortalized by Bradley Cooper in the Clint Eastwood film *American Sniper*. The sleepy brick buildings downtown, large, overpriced McMansions surrounding it, and . . . not much else had always made Midlothian a less-than-perfect cultural fit for Emily's nontraditional sensibilities. But it was a good place to raise her kids, at least. It was too conservative, too judgmental, and too homogenously white by her standards, but it felt safe. Her fellow Midlothians maintained their distance for the most part, seeing her tattoos as a warning sign of trouble, but that didn't bother her, and she mostly kept to herself anyway. Her three young kids, caring for her father at home, and online college studies kept her busy enough.

But Emily does like to drive fast. Too fast. Or at least she did when she still had her own car and a driver's license. She piled up a double-digit–sized collection of speeding tickets over the course of just a few years around North Texas. This was a decade before I spoke with her, when she was in her early twenties and, as she described herself, young and dumb. At first, she tried to pay off some of the tickets, but as they stacked up and the fees for not paying them sprouted like weeds, she started ignoring the mounting debt. It was too much trouble to deal with and easier to not think about it. After all, they were just some speeding tickets.

What was the worst that could happen for driving too fast, too often, and not paying off the fines? As we chatted over Zoom, I found myself thinking that Emily's story wasn't all that hard to imagine. A small town, fast cars, a punitive justice system that doesn't much care about offenders beyond retribution and collecting fines. I met Emily through her attorney and a program that worked with people to get arduous court fines reduced. We spoke at length online and by phone, and her story taught me a lot about how desperation can push people into selling their blood plasma.

When Emily was told she might go to jail for all those unpaid fines, she checked in with the courthouse and found a raft of tickets, some of them written at places she had never even visited. She couldn't figure out how she could possibly have amassed so many outstanding fines and fees, their collective weight spiraling ever more out of her control. It seemed like a cruel glitch in the court's computer system, but she was in way over her head and fixing all the problems felt impossible. By that time, she had lost her driver's license because of too many traffic tickets. But daily life in Texas was impossible without a car, so she kept driving, and the tickets became more expensive, the fees grew higher, and the hole she dug grew even deeper.

I was initially connected to Emily's attorney through Alec Karakatsanis, a civil rights lawyer, social justice advocate, and cofounder of the nonprofit Equal Justice Under Law. In 2016, his group won a landmark court settlement in Jennings, Missouri, about the town's long-standing practice of throwing people into the city jail for unpaid fines and for fees on petty infractions like traffic tickets. A court awarded more than 2,000 people in the town a total of $4.7 million, agreeing that repeatedly jailing citizens over small charges was a practice that needed to change. That lawsuit said that the courts in Jennings, with fewer than 15,000 residents, routinely issued more warrants than the number of households that existed in the town, and that they were most often issued for traffic violations. Residents who got pulled over for speeding had a decent chance of ending up in the local jail at some point, especially if they were not able to stay on top of the fines and fees. In a lot of cases like that, people will sell their plasma to pay off the fees. The expenses pile up, and selling plasma is an easy, quick way to earn some money.

Being poor is expensive. Costly errors add up. Making even a minor mistake if you're a person who lacks resources can trap you financially for years. In fact, the system often seems designed to keep people mired in poverty, making it impossible to climb out and penalizing the most those who have the least. Some states have tried to do away with the worst, most punitive parts of the fee system, like the recent de facto ending of cash bail in New Jersey and Alaska, and an experimental program to do the same in Montana. But for the most part, and in most places, and certainly in conservative Midlothian, Texas, the system remains largely unreformed and totally dependent on the whims of local officials.

———

Emily tried to set up a plan with the court to slowly pay off her bills each month, but that didn't work, either. The fees kept adding up, making the total seem insurmountable. Eventually, the crisis came to a head. Emily lived through what she remembers as a nightmare when she was pulled over by police, handcuffed, and arrested on an outstanding warrant for unpaid traffic tickets, all in front of her terrified, crying children. She had always taught her kids that police officers were the good guys and the bad guys were the people they arrested. So how was she going to explain to them that she might be on the wrong side of all that? She remembered this as a moment of panic and despair, the worst moment of her life.

When the crisis passed, she once again attempted to sort it all out, working methodically to pay off the fines and fees bit by bit—or at least the ones she could locate in the county's computer system. As her debt pile shrank a little, she began to feel like her errors might be fading away. Years went by without further incident, and Emily thought she was on the road back to normal. But then disaster struck once more.

Emily is drawn to unusual people—friends who don't always conform to what passes as acceptable in her affluent, largely white town. A few years into her relative normality, she found herself riding in a car with one of those quirky friends, a bit of an oddball whose personality, she said in hindsight, was likely amplified by recreational drug use. When the police pulled them over, the incident ended with Emily being slapped with a more serious charge. In that moment she moved into a less forgiving level of the criminal justice system. "I gave up on the idea of ever being able to drive again," Emily remembered. "I would go to work and end up getting another ticket."

With the traffic incident, Emily, a single mom, had gone from living with a long history of bothersome traffic tickets to having a real charge, one that could derail her life for years. She was given a deferred sentence and put on probation, which meant even more fees owed to the Texas court system, with potentially worse repercussions. She said her probation officer suggested she use her child-support payments to pay the fees. When I spoke with her, Emily half joked about her solitary life, saying she had few friends left because she just could not trust people like she used to.

———

There were few options in Emily's small town for decent paid work, and she was in school and raising children. She jumped at the chance when a friend told her she could earn hundreds of dollars each month by selling her blood plasma. That's how she ended up catching rides with a friend, or her dad, to the next town, so she could have a thick needle stuck in the crook of her arm, often two times a week, to earn money to pay back the courts. She did it for two years, until she had to stop during the COVID pandemic, earning money to the tune of more than $2,000 dollars, all of which has gone toward paying down what once seemed to be an insurmount-able pile of fines and fees.

As we chatted, I struggled at times to keep up with Emily's cha-otic story of descent into enormous debt. It's certainly a lot to follow, and I got lost more than once and had to go back and have her retell the details. She was open about it all, though, and did not hide the fact that she had made mistakes. Her grievance lies in the impossi-bility of repairing those mistakes and moving on with her life.

In our conversations, I heard someone who found it easier to ig-nore what was piling up than to address it, and a complicated series of bad decisions that stacked up, each one adding to a pile of prob-lems that could derail her entire life. But I now understood the allure of selling plasma for someone like Emily, who had been saddled with the pressures of our fee-based criminal justice system, and with kids to raise and a record that put traditional employment just beyond her reach. Plasma seemed like one of the only ways she might dig herself out of a seemingly bottomless hole. Now she has a hole in her arm—that deep telltale scar—to show for it all.

But Emily found that even the easy money from selling plasma had its challenges. She did not have a car or an active driver's li-cense, so she remained dependent on other people to get anywhere. If she could have driven herself, she would have gone to the plasma center twice a week to make as much money as possible, but she couldn't. Because her dad was a busy school principal, he couldn't always take time away to drive her during business hours. Getting a ride an hour each way from someone who could also wait for her or pick her up when she finished proved difficult. With the arrival of the COVID-19 pandemic, she quit relying on the plasma money tap, afraid to be exposed to the virus at that packed plasma center and potentially passing the illness on to her dad or her kids.

Emily would go back to the plasma center tomorrow, though, if it were a more convenient option. Nothing else was available for her to make money in the same way. "If I had my own transportation, I probably would, because I need that $75. I know it's an amazing thing, but it does physically exhaust me," she told me. "I would sell my kidney if I could have, in order to pay for probation."

There was a glimmer of humor in Emily's response, but I knew she was serious. She learned that her driving habits would only exacerbate her problems, but finding alternatives to paid plasma led to dead ends. "I'm thankful and grateful it's a possibility," she told me. "Sometimes there's nothing else we can do."

Prison Blood

In Alec Karakatsanis's work with people like Emily, people who wind up on the wrong side of the criminal justice system, he often hears from criminal defendants forced to take extreme measures to pay fines and fees. He told me this can mean selling blood plasma as a device to stay out of jail. The pressure to sell blood plasma, or do whatever else it takes to make money, rarely comes as an overt order from judges or probation officers, but Karakatsanis said the next time that explicit advice is offered, it won't be the first. Mostly, in places like the rural American South, defendants learn through a word-of-mouth network that selling their plasma can be the proverbial golden ticket out of the fines and fees inherent in modern criminal justice. Karakatsanis hears from clients who say it's a common practice in states like Alabama and Missouri, and in jurisdictions like Michigan and Ohio, where court fees tend to run higher and criminal defendants get into truly desperate financial situations. "People in these communities go to the plasma centers because they don't have money in general," he told me.

Karakatsanis pointed me to an especially egregious case in Alabama reported by the *New York Times* in 2015. Marvin Wiggins, a longtime circuit court judge in rural Alabama, drew heat from the community when it emerged that he had demanded that defendants in his court donate blood as part of paying their debt to society. Judges do all kinds of wacky things in smaller jurisdictions that pass without notice, but this one attracted national attention. Hundreds of people facing charges for crimes like hunting after dark, passing bad checks, and drug possession in Judge Wiggins's court were told that if they didn't have money, they could show up with receipts for blood donations, and their fines and fees would be reduced by $100 each. The judge didn't push people directly into selling plasma at a for-profit company clinic, but he did offer to reduce costs for those offenders who gave up blood as an altruistic endeavor. In this context, as the head of a courtroom and in communication with a defendant already under personal distress, the judge gave them little choice but to say yes. Unless they were wealthy, which most people in these circumstances are not. It was, experts agreed, both unprecedented and inappropriate.

A defendant in Judge Wiggins's courtroom one day recorded what the judge said:

> For your consideration, there's a blood drive outside and if you do not have any money and you don't want to go to jail, as an option to pay it, you can give blood today. If you do not have any money, go out there and give blood and bring in a receipt indicating you gave blood. Consider that as a discount rather than putting you in jail, if you do not have any money. So, if you do not have any money and you don't want to go to jail, consider giving blood today and bring your receipt back, or the sheriff has enough handcuffs for those who do not have money.

Judge Wiggins was charged with ethics violations, suspended, and publicly censured for the actions recorded in that trial. And yet, despite having been investigated for this and other improprieties as a judge over the years, he remains on the bench.

Wiggins's bizarre demand that defendants give up their blood might just be seen as a singular high-profile example of malfeasance, but the links connecting the histories of blood extraction and the criminal justice system are inexorable and strong. In a similar instance in the 1960s, Arkansas began to engineer a paid blood extraction program involving prison inmates that turned deadly and has largely been forgotten by history. Over the course of twenty years, the state prison system implemented a plan to sign a contract with Health Management Associates (HMA), a Little Rock biomedical company. HMA agreed to pay prison inmates a pittance for their blood plasma, which was then sold to pharmaceutical companies for $50 per "donation." Half the proceeds went back into the coffers of the Arkansas correctional system, while the company kept the rest.

Prison systems in other places have dabbled in similar schemes to monetize the blood of their inmates, but they gave way when complaints piled up. The prison plasma plots tended to involve areas with larger minority populations, exploiting people with less power to fight back. But no other place has gone bigger or more aggressive on prisoner blood, with more disastrous results, than Arkansas. Multiple news accounts in Arkansas from the 1980s and early '90s described how state prison inmates were not *forced* to sell their plasma, but it was the only way they could make money. The inmates filed into massive state-owned gyms, lay down on ramshackle cots, and had their veins tapped as if it were a job. The concept was normalized.

Journalist Mara Leveritt of the *Arkansas Times* described the bizarre scene in a 1991 report:

> *After passing a few blood tests, prisoners were paid $7 per visit to lie in one of the [Arkansas Department of Corrections'] two gymnasium-sized plasmapheresis centers and bleed out their valuable plasma. Since inmates are not paid for their prison jobs, plasma was the only legal way for them to make money to spend on extras like toiletries. The program was a small windfall for the department as well, helping the ADC retain one of the lowest average inmate-cost-per-day figures in the nation.*

Given the state of medical science regarding blood-borne diseases at the time, and the newness of the global plasma trade, the Arkansas prisoners were not strictly screened for diseases. Medical science was just beginning to grapple with the risks of HIV and AIDS. Multiple investigations by journalists and governmental agencies have since linked HIV-contaminated blood from Arkansas to HIV infections in other countries, acquired through tainted blood sold in medical products. It was another piece in the puzzle of how HIV spread through medicines sold around the globe.

I've never found precise documentation that connects this to Arkansas prison blood, but it was around this time—1985—that China banned the import of foreign blood products, writing off the HIV crisis as a foreign illness and turning me into a blood smuggler a couple of decades later. Transmission was a hazy subject when researchers were just beginning to understand the virus that causes AIDS—that it was carried in the blood and transmitted to others as the blood moved from one body into another. As warnings began to surface in the 1980s about prison-harvested blood carrying a higher risk of contamination with HIV and hepatitis, the FDA ordered American drugmakers to stop using the raw plasma of prisoners. During this era, before science caught up with viral transmission, thousands of Americans, including children, had contracted the virus through blood-derived medications. Even after safeguards were developed, for a short time, tainted blood from the United States was still sold around the world.

In 2003, a group of hemophiliacs who contracted HIV through tainted blood products sued Cutter Laboratories, a division of Bayer pharmaceuticals, for knowingly selling contaminated blood on the global market. In documents produced in court, the plaintiffs alleged that Cutter, a company later bought by Bayer, knew it was selling potentially dangerous stock, but some medical communities outside the United States were unaware of the risks. American doctors knew how HIV was spread, as the research was mainly done in the United States; public health leaders elsewhere had less access to the latest science about the virus. By 2011, Bayer had paid out millions to settle the legal claims from around the globe. Their decision not to use prison blood spared many in this country but killed others living in places less protected by their medical systems.

The emergence of stories about contaminated American blood set loose in Asia and South America begat years of investigations, allegations of cover-ups, and links to widespread illness and death from infected plasma sold worldwide. Arkansas finally ended its prison blood-for-profit program in 1994, but only after it had left a long trail of victims around the globe. The fact that former president Bill Clinton was governor of Arkansas during the worst years of the state's blood scandal has perhaps contributed to the relative silence regarding the state's role in the blood disaster, as attempts to talk about it even now can feel politicized. But for hemophiliacs and others who depended on plasma-made medications and contracted HIV and AIDS in the process, and for those with rare illnesses like my own who need plasma, the consequences were real and sometimes fatal. At the time, hemophilia was the primary disease treated with

human blood products; this was before the widespread use of IVIG—
the drug I use—and before other biologics made from human blood
became much more common. A Canadian government investigation
eventually found that infected batches of Arkansas prison plasma had
wound up with health-care providers and were used by patients in
fourteen countries, including Canada, Switzerland, and Japan.

Poisoned Exports

After many failed efforts, I eventually met one of the 1,800 people
in Japan who was infected with HIV from the tainted global blood
supply chain. It's hard not to see this story as one of exploitation
and failure, from beginning to end. The victims who died through
this slice of the plasma economy largely didn't understand how it
had happened or what kind of simple procedures could have been
used to protect them from the infections, let alone receive an ethical response from the supplier. The legacy of this for me and others
dependent on blood products has been stricter donor screening and
a ban on blood plasma from gay men—the latter a relic from a time
when discriminatory practices that target people based on sexual
orientation were accepted as necessity.

It's been decades, and many have forgotten the U.S. blood-pool
scandal of the AIDS era, but its stigma lingers in strange and punitive
ways. When I was in Tokyo in 2015, I met with one of the estimated
1,800 people in Japan who had been infected with HIV from tainted
U.S. blood products. I had read about this man earlier and went to
meet him in his grand office at the Japanese Diet, or parliament. It
took a lot of wrangling to arrange the meeting. I would later learn
that this period is a chapter in Japan's recent history that most prefer
to conceal. We sat across from one another at a large oak table and I
watched him while he told me his story of how plasma gone wrong
had come to define his life.

Ryuhei Kawada was diagnosed with hemophilia—a blood clotting disorder—shortly after he was born. Advances in medical
science—the development of a drug that worked to stave off cease-
less bleeding—at that time allowed him to enjoy a relatively normal
childhood. Kawada carved out his normalcy with regular injections
of a medication that is one of the most common products made from

human blood. As he described what happened to him as a child, he rubbed the back of one hand, tracing the spot where needles for years had pierced his skin and a vein to deliver his lifesaving drug. I recognized the action because I often do the same when I talk about my own infusions. Speaking about the needle going in can spark an involuntary reaction—the need to protect and remember the spot where the syringe has invaded your body.

In Kawada's case, the drug that sustained him contained what might have been a deadly payload, if he hadn't been luckier than others in his situation. At the age of 10, in the late 1980s, he was diagnosed with HIV. He lived in secret with that diagnosis for years, but eventually he decided he should not feel ashamed. Instead, he told me how he and his family wanted the people whose negligence had left him infected with the virus to own up to their mistake.

With the public and private support of his mother, he became one of the first people in Japan to publicly disclose his HIV diagnosis, a cultural breakthrough in a country where the disease was especially stigmatized. Kawada joined a lawsuit against his country's blood bank and six drug companies that supplied unsafe plasma-based medicine, an event in Japan's recent history so disturbing that it is today rarely spoken of in public or media.

Although he seemed quite willing to talk about living with HIV and suing the Japanese government, the group I worked with in Japan had quietly cautioned me against bringing it up. But we talked about it at length. Years earlier, Kawada's advocacy for patient rights had rocked the foundations of power and led to high-profile resignations. It also spurred Kawada to adopt a life and career as an activist, which he continues today as a member of Japan's Constitutional Democratic Party.

In a strange twist, a few years after our meeting, I watched a musical in Los Angeles based on his life and his role in Japan as a public face of the HIV crisis. Singing doctors and patients danced their way through a cross-border blood crisis. Later came the parallel that Wang Shuping, the Chinese whistleblower I had met a few years earlier, also had her life story told onstage. I don't know why, perhaps it's a fascination with the macabre, but big blood debacles seem to inspire theater productions. Maybe the abject strangeness of it all translates well to the stage.

In our conversation in Tokyo, Kawada spoke of the dual stigmas that marked his life, first hemophilia and then HIV. He remembered the details clearly, recounting the moments in his quiet and deliberate way. In both events, he was expected to hide his "weakness" from society, but he eventually refused to do so. This, too, is familiar to me as an American. Our society views illness and disability as weaknesses, in ways that are made manifest in discrimination, from health care to employment. For most of my adult life, I've felt compelled to hide the fact that I have a chronic condition that could disable me if left untreated. Until recently, I've told only close friends and family. I know intuitively that sharing this part of myself will shut off work opportunities, innately change people's view of me, and mark me as someone lesser in the eyes of other Americans.

We often think better of ourselves, but I see the reminders every day. I can tell when a person's first response to learning of my chronic illness is "You don't look sick." I don't even know what that means anymore. Most of the time, I look and feel like anyone else. But on harder days, that isn't the case. On those days, I *do* look sick—when my legs don't work quite right and I walk with a shuffle or a dropped toe that catches the edge of a stair.

Plasma sellers in the United States, and even people who donate for free, these days are questioned at length and their blood is tested before their cells are accepted. In the 1980s, medical science evolved to learn that simply treating human plasma with extreme heat after it is extracted kills HIV, hepatitis, and other blood-borne viruses. But in lawsuits filed since the 1980s in regard to the HIV blood scandal, plaintiffs in Japan and elsewhere charge that the American drug company Cutter, later bought by Bayer, knowingly dumped untreated, HIV-laden blood outside the United States. Kawada was one of the lucky ones who survived, a victim who lived to tell his story and spread the word about those who had endangered thousands. Kawada's lifework as a truth-teller and activist is a rare bright spot in the dark tale of the global blood economy.

Yes, the viral dangers in blood when it's moved from one body to another have been largely eliminated. Our American system of predatory imbalances, the overarching trait that caused prison inmates to be leeched by industry, persists. What hasn't yet been fixed, or even much addressed, is the growing number and persistent invisibility of people in the American criminal justice system who are pushed to their ends, selling pieces of themselves—up to and including their blood—for a pittance so as to dig their way out of financial holes.

Digging Out

Talking with Emily about her court fines and fees brought that into focus for me. Our first time speaking to each other took place with her lawyer also on the Zoom call. The second time, over the phone, was just the two of us. She was fine with me using her real name, unlike many plasma sellers I met, because she genuinely doesn't believe it's anything for her to be ashamed of. I told her I agree, and she's one of the few donors who did not seem too weirded out when I told her some of her plasma might have found its way into my veins.

Back in Midlothian, Texas, Emily spent her days online in her virtual classrooms, writing papers and planning her future, a future free of the endless grind she had been put through by the Texas criminal justice system. Like so many people I have met selling their plasma, Emily had the telltale permanent divot in the crook of one arm—for her, it was a war wound from paying off debts that seemed like they might never disappear. But unlike most, Emily's scar covered another layer of burden. It's not just from being broke; for her, it was a reminder of the biggest mistakes of her life, namely the drug arrest during her wayward car ride. While college students and middle-class people sell their plasma to boost their budgets, people caught in the criminal justice system face nothing but impossible choices. I've never doubted that when she told me she'd sell an organ if she could, she meant it. Emily is in a better place now, but her blood-money scar is a dual stigma she'll place atop the pile for the rest of her life. As I went deeper into Texas, I began to learn how the blood trade crosses international lines and targets even more economically vulnerable people.

CHAPTER 13
Borderlands

The border is a rusted hinge that does not bend.
The border is the blood clot in the river's vein.
—Alberto Ríos

B orders reveal our deepest chasms. If you want to see inequality distilled to its barest form, head straight to the U.S.-Mexico border, the dividing line between American myth and legend, replete with genuine inclusive patriotism and the darkest pits of bigotry. It is the best of ourselves and the worst. Most Americans hear about the borderlands from far away, every two or four years when national elections bring them to the front, with racism and xenophobia on full display. The border looms large in the imaginations of people who have never seen it. But the people who live along the border year-round have more complex, more interesting lives than what is portrayed during campaign season. The border delineates and sustains economic imbalances, yet across it, for many years, has flowed one of the largest, most reliable streams of blood sellers who feed the global plasma industry.

In 2020, I first went to the Texas borderlands to meet people who crossed international lines to sell their blood plasma to pay their bills, and to study the unique proposition of navigating that life in El Paso. It's a West Texas city that hugs the curve of the U.S. border with Mexico, a place where you can see into the hearts of both countries at the same time. El Paso is a vibrant place, filled with colorful buildings and homes flanked by the craggy, dry Franklin Mountains, south of the Rockies and not part of that long chain I drove alongside to get here. The city's artists have made its streets and buildings into their canvases, painting vibrant murals of heroes and historic events that bring the region's stories to life. In Lincoln Park, which runs under a busy tangle of roads, images of Martin Luther King Jr. and Frida Kahlo adorn concrete pillars at a much larger-than-life scale.

It's a city that can be a little confusing at first to an outsider like me. For instance, it is difficult to make out where one city ends and the next begins, until you see the clear, snaking divide and notice how the Rio Grande and a long, coppery brown fence separate the American city of El Paso from the Mexican metropolis of Juárez. In many ways these two desert cities, separated by a river and a border, function as one metropolis yet are worlds apart economically. For years, the river bridges were crossings where people on the lower end of the economic ladder were drawn to what seemed like an easy way to make money.

El Paso was built in the 1850s as a stagecoach stop on the route west to California. If any city can lay claim to being a picture-perfect version of the rugged Old West, El Paso is probably it. Its brick and adobe buildings in a downtown preserved in time give the place the feel of a movie set. El Paso is in Texas, but it is a distinctly Mexican city. People here are charming, warm, and immensely proud of their city. Knowing its history helps explains the city's unusual position on the U.S. map. El Paso lives in the far corner of the westernmost point of Texas. The city is positioned just south of New Mexico and minutes from Juárez—much closer to both than it is any other major Texas city.

This corner of the world has long been one of travel and trade, from the Indigenous people of the area to the descendants of settlers, cowboys, and today's busy businesspeople. El Paso has just under 700,000 residents, 82 percent of whom identify as Hispanic or Latinx—the second-highest percentage in the country, behind only McAllen, Texas, to the southeast. It is also a Democratic Party stronghold in this state known for far-right politics. El Paso is an unusual place, full of Wild West history and a present shaped by the unrelenting political attacks against its neighbors to the south and the American citizens who have roots there of their own.

Across the border, and visible from most of El Paso, lies Ciudad

Juárez, the biggest city in the Mexican state of Chihuahua. Named for a former president of Mexico, Juárez carries the burden of an international reputation for gang and drug cartel violence. In the mid-2000s, a spike in murders here drew international attention. Violence against women has been especially rampant in the city. In the three years leading up to 2021, nearly 500 women were murdered in Juárez, a shocking spate of violence that led authorities in the Mexican city to issue a first-of-its-kind gender violence alert. The region is dangerous for local journalists, too, and making a living in Juárez can be tough.

Crossing the border to sell plasma for some cash, in comparison to the surrounding conditions for those making the trek into El Paso, might not seem like that big a deal. Most people I met and interviewed who make that trip were unfazed by that portion of their lives, much in keeping with a pattern I found all around the country for those who sell plasma. When I've mentioned my travels to friends and family who live wealthier lives in New York, Montana, and elsewhere, the idea of selling blood elicits an immediate and unmistakable recoil. But in places where material conditions are imperfect, the psychological barrier to entry to selling their plasma feels like not much of a hurdle at all. In places like Flint, Rexburg, and Juárez, scarcity proves to be the unfortunate motivator. But among the many people I've interviewed who sell plasma, they rarely have the time to consider long-term health implications; blood sellers typically don't live lives that afford the luxury of asking why it doesn't pay more or what the practice might do to their bodies. Their concerns are much more immediate.

The cities of El Paso, Juárez, and nearby Las Cruces, New Mexico, fifty miles north, account for a thriving metropolitan area of 2.7 million people. On my map of plasma extraction centers around the country, this region is a hot spot, with clusters of red dots. There are plasma clinics throughout the area. But, as with most of the rest of the world, how you fare in those cities depends on nothing so much as where you were born. Thousands of Mexican citizens cross the border every day from Juárez for work, for school, to visit family on the other side of the river in El Paso. It's a short distance to cross from one country to the other and back—twenty minutes to walk across one bridge from Juárez to El Paso, and only a few minutes' drive across another. But it could take hours when the U.S. border guards were being difficult. When the crossings were busy, waits could stretch even longer as the guards grew more hostile, less patient, more intimidating.

————

I first visited the borderlands to take in El Paso's blood-selling scene one month before the World Health Organization declared the novel coronavirus a global pandemic in March 2020. Back then, cross-border traffic was brisk, with more than 1,000 people crossing each day to refill the international blood-plasma pool. Few of the people I met and spoke with showed much concern about getting busted at the border; the plasma centers themselves were insistent about keeping the flow moving, telling donors the practice was fine and they were not doing anything illegal by crossing over to sell plasma. But only a few weeks after I visited and saw the free flow, the United States closed its border with Mexico, leaving the land boundary shuttered for more than a year and a half for most people who traveled overland. Conveniently enough, people who had more money—tourists and business travelers—were allowed to fly in and out of Mexico. The land border—where working-class people, who required U.S. entry to pay their bills and support loved ones in Mexico—was shut down.

I returned a second time to El Paso in 2021. I had flown the first time, but on the way back, I drove to avoid the pandemic risks of being stuck in an airplane with other people. I followed the spine of the Rocky Mountains south through Idaho, Utah, New Mexico, and into this slivered outland of Texas. On the road to El Paso, I stopped to see plasma extraction centers in the bigger cities of Idaho Falls and Salt Lake City along the way. They were always busy.

The landscape of the U.S. Southwest changes as you near the border; it's wider, drier. Sometimes I'm embarrassed that my home state has claimed Big Sky Country as its nickname, because I've seen bigger skies. This is one of those. The blood sellers from Mexico crossed the border beneath awe-inspiring heavens to make their lives a little easier, but as always, I wondered at what cost to their own lives.

For years, the American borderlands have been the absolute heart of global blood plasma extraction, adding immense amounts to the giant pool of blood plasma. A 2019 investigative report from ProPublica and ARD, Germany's public television network, first brought me to this area to witness the large scale of one of the bigger clusters of paid-plasma centers. The network obtained confidential documents from a global plasma company based in Europe that revealed the industry's borderland clinics are the most productive in the world. The investigation estimated that 10,000 Mexican citizens crossed the border into the United States each week to sell their plasma to one of five Grifols border plasma centers, which then turned their blood cells into the medical equivalent of liquid gold. At that time, for some residents of Juárez, the $400 a month they could make—at the absolute maximum—was a better salary than that offered for jobs they could find back home. For others, the plasma selling was a hefty supplemental income. The minimum wage in Juárez at that time was $12.50 per day, the equivalent of just over $3,250 for a full year of work.

The targeting of the U.S.-Mexico borderlands aligns with what I have seen in other parts of the country, from Idaho to Michigan and beyond. While the industry disputes the claim that its practices are predatory, my maps don't lie. There are more plasma centers in places with economic precarity. Along the U.S. border with Mexico, there were forty-three plasma centers when I made the trip. The documents ARD cited in their report said those centers are "the most productive" in the United States, and the United States is the world's largest supplier of blood plasma.

Border officials were reluctant to say whether the plasma-industry payments to Mexican citizens violated visa rules, but before the practice was shut down, plasma sellers were advised to keep to themselves their reasons for crossing into the United States. One plasma seller told me he never got specific instructions from the donation center, "but everyone knows about it." Some cross-border plasma sellers said plasma center staff would tell them exactly what documents to bring.

It was an open secret as to who filled the plasma pools on the border, and officials who policed the frontier appeared to be part of the charade. Before the border closed, the centers were so flush with donors and plasma that local news reports indicated the border closure led, in part, to a months-long shortage of plasma supplies in the United States. The sudden decision to ban the cross-border donors threatened to reduce the profits of major international companies that depend on the blood of people who need the cash they get by selling it. Before the border agency made its decision to ban the practice in 2021, with little warning, blood sellers lived in a gray area for years when they crossed into the United States to fill up the IV bags at plasma centers with their cells.

————

My first stop on that initial trip to El Paso was a CSL Behring plasma extraction center in a strip mall near the University of Texas at El Paso. I had plotted out a route to the plasma centers on my phone, and I spent the day driving from one center to the next to see how busy they were. In this CSL center, there was a donor appreciation party going on, with '80s rock music blaring into the parking lot from the sidewalk outside the center. The staff handed out hot dogs and sodas to people as they left the center, many of the donors pouring ketchup and mustard on the buns with one hand and the other hand holding or adjusting the tight band of adhesive strapped around their arms to stop the holes from bleeding. Even with the music and snacks, it just didn't seem all that much fun. People looked tired and hungry, sating their post-donation appetite with the free meal on the sidewalk.

Outside the center, I spoke with a handful of donors who were heading back to their cars or walking to the bus stop. A few lived in El Paso, while several others lived across the border in Juárez. Most of them were in a hurry to get home; it was hot and they were tired. I stood around outside in the parking lot like a survey taker, stopping people on their way out of the door. Several told me they didn't want to talk at all—more so than at centers in the other cities I had visited. I assumed their reluctance had to do with the fuzzy legal area in which they existed—crossing the border to sell plasma and earning money off the grid.

When I returned to El Paso more than a year after that first visit, deep into the heart of the pandemic's second bruising year, the land border was still closed. All along El Paso's downtown sidewalks and city streets, banners pleaded with the locals to sell their plasma. It was clear the borderland plasma clinics' traffic had tanked. The companies offered high bonuses to draw in U.S. residents, who weren't filling the plasma bags to the same degree as their Mexican counterparts. As I walked along an empty downtown sidewalk, on a street that would have taken me right to the border if I kept going, I noticed the going rates advertised for selling plasma were higher. A familiar wave rushed over me as I walked along, the chill of knowing that my ability to walk depended on people being desperate enough to go for that extra cash.

When the border closure stopped Mexican citizens from crossing over, plasma extraction companies began offering up to $1,500 or $1,600 a month for regular donors—more than what they had advertised just a year before, when plenty of Mexican citizens still filled their chairs. The higher payout was alluring, but their reliable pool had dried up. With the land border still shut to people traveling by foot and car, I took to making telephone calls with the assistance of Verónica Martínez, an investigative journalist who lives on the Mexican side of the border, in Juárez. She had no trouble finding people who sold their plasma in Texas. She spoke with several donors and then helped me arrange a series of phone calls so I could hear their stories. Through them, I learned something else was afoot.

Over crackling phone lines, I talked with donors who live in Juárez, who described a range of experiences in the blood trade. I spoke through a translator for some of the interviews, but it worked well enough to hear their stories. I wanted to know what had drawn them across the border to sell plasma, if it was worth it, and if they would come back if they could. Their experiences came before the pandemic, when it was still easy to cross over and the blood trade was appealing. Nearly all the people I spoke with saw the plasma economy with some suspicion, but they took part in it.

Several people said they had been hearing rumors for months that they would no longer be allowed to donate in the United States, so they had not bothered to try again. It was a hassle, and as it did to most other people in the world, the pandemic forced them to get by with less and to reduce their living expenses.

A man I'll call David, who was 39 when we spoke, was born in Ciudad Juárez but lived in the United States from elementary school through his early twenties. When his visa expired and he was unable to renew it in 2010, he moved back to Mexico. Right away, life was more difficult because of the huge drop in his standard of living. The shift was immense, he said, not just for the culture shock but also the shock to his finances. He was able to earn only a fraction of what he had made in the United States, even while working as a supervisor at a Juárez factory. He began selling his plasma in El Paso, going at least four times a month to make up for the decline in his income, earning as much as $600 each month. David described the cross-border plasma experience as "easy money," and he kept it up for two years. All you had to do, he said, was lie back in the chair and relax while the plasma flowed. The needles didn't bother him at all, and he felt fine physically. The tricky part was getting over the border.

The border crossings are often clogged with long lines of cars and people moving back and forth between Mexico and Texas. Plasma sellers told me how waiting at the border, not knowing whether the guards would hassle them about why they were crossing over, added to their concerns. I remember the anxiety that washed over me every time I returned to China with the illicit blood-based medication in my luggage. Would this be the time I got caught? But I did that only a couple times a year, not twice a week, and I could have left China and moved back home if I wanted to. My entire income did not depend on keeping the game going. For Mexicans crossing into the United States, the stakes are much higher.

David and other plasma donors who came into the United States to sell their blood parts have told me that the plasma centers deliberately targeted their advertising and instructions at them, eschewing any concerns about legal or ethical matters regarding donations from givers based outside the United States. The centers advertised in Mexico that it was safe and legal; in a later court case they contended that it had been an accepted practice for thirty years. It was a strange, hazy area to exist in, but David never had any real trouble with the border guards. To make sure it remained so, he lied if they asked why he was crossing, telling them he was going to see family or do some shopping. After two years of regular trips back and forth across the border, he found a better job working as a supervisor at another factory in Juárez, which enabled him to stop giving blood for profit. The money offered in the El Paso center made the trips no longer worth the hassle, but he did not regret having done it, nor is he ashamed. Blood money gave him enough freedom to find a comfortable living back in Mexico—it was a cushion.

Whatever deliberate, market-based formula companies use to determine how much they will pay plasma sellers must somehow calculate the hassle factor. Many people I've met described how they finally quit selling plasma when the money was no longer worth the inconveniences. They are usually replaced with new plasma sellers, but there is a point when the headaches outweigh the rewards. For college students in Rexburg, the down-and-out in Flint, and the people of Juárez, maybe that point comes a little later than in places like Salt Lake City or Missoula. The line might be when the physical exhaustion, the commute, the time spent waiting in line, or the simple annoyance at getting stuck by a large needle so many times that it leaves a permanent crater in your arm becomes too much. The wear on a person grows with the weeks and months and years.

In many cases, here just as everywhere else, selling plasma was a kind of crazy thing people needed to do in college, they said, but it just wasn't worth doing when living in the adult world. While the industry does prey on poverty and inequality, as spelled out in the brisk plasma trade on the border, it seems it did not pay enough to keep most people on the donor rolls for more than a few years. People like David find better jobs, others finish paying off their student or medical debts, and many more simply age out of selling plasma. This is what I've heard across the country. It gets old, and plasma sellers get tired of the drag. The system depends on a steady churn of younger, newer suppliers who need money.

———

For Mariana (not her real name) who is in her late twenties and lives in Juárez, the difficulty of the endeavor was never worth the money. In 2017, she heard about the possibility of making money by selling plasma from a college friend who did it on a regular basis. The friend was encouraged to recruit her with the promise of a bonus, and she sold Mariana on the idea. Mariana does not like needles, but she agreed to go, in part to help her friend and hoping she would be able to overcome her anxiety at being stuck. Mariana said the undertaking, including crossing the border, waiting to be processed into the system, and making the donation itself, made her nauseous, and by the time her turn came, she was hungry and stuck in a chair for an hour while the machine extracted her blood.

The pay sounded good at first—earning up to $50 or even $100 in the beginning stages—but unlike the rising price per donation I saw in pandemic-era Rexburg, Mariana found that pay decreased the longer you continued. The high rates advertised to draw people in the door dropped when the person became a frequent donor. She went back a handful of times, but the money never made up for the difficulty of getting to the center or the ill feeling that selling plasma gave her. There were just too many bad situations adding up, Mariana said. It wasn't worth it for $25.

Mariana went back to the plasma-selling business about a year later, when she and some friends were saving up for a trip to Disneyland over summer break. She needed an extra $300 to cover expenses for the vacation and went to the plasma center exactly enough times to get the money she needed. She had since become a working professional; she was making enough money that selling plasma seemed far from her day-to-day reality. When she thought back on it, she recalled a friend who had deep scars on her arm from selling plasma often for several years.

Yes, the cost of living in Mexico is much less than in the United States, but blood is still blood. A person's body is worth more than top-ups on a debit card. With the way she felt after selling plasma, Mariana worried about the long-term impact on a donor's health, and she wondered if there was something the companies don't tell donors about the risks. It felt unrealistic to her that removing a critical bodily fluid with such regularity could possibly be a healthy, unharmful endeavor.

Mariana wouldn't recommend it. She said she knows it is for a good cause, and they tell you everything they do with plasma, but a lot of people don't care about that. They do it for the money alone.

And the money was a sure bet for three decades, until the trade shut down overnight.

CHAPTER 14
A Battle for Blood on the Border

Selling plasma constitutes
labor for hire.
—U.S. Customs and Border Protection

At first, Gabriel—not his real name—thought the endeavor sounded like a scam, but he tried it anyway. He began selling plasma in El Paso in 2019, when he was in his early twenties. He would wake up in Juárez by 7 a.m., leave his house by 8 a.m., then ride two public buses to get to the Bridge of the Americas, a hulking iron span across the Rio Grande with eight lanes of traffic and flanked by footpaths. The bridge carries the highest volume of U.S.–Mexico traffic of any border crossing. In normal times, thousands of people move back and forth every day.

For Gabriel, the easiest way into the United States was to walk across the bridge and through the checkpoint, where he would answer a few questions and show his paperwork to enter the United States. From there, he walked a few more blocks along El Paso's streets, past food markets, bars, clusters of quaint little shops, and restaurants, to the downtown CSL Plasma extraction center. When it went smoothly, he could be back home in Juárez, flush with extra cash from his plasma donation, by noon. He got used to it and continued walking over the bridge across the Rio Grande to donate, often twice a week, usually five times a month or more, to supplement his family's income.

His trek to sell blood was a common one, even routine for many, but when a U.S. government agency put a surprise stop to the practice in 2021, the blood of people like Gabriel became the focus of an international legal fight. The battle revealed just how important the blood plasma of Mexican citizens is in the global trade.

On my first trip to El Paso back in early 2020, I had seen the brigade of border crossers who sold plasma. They arrived in the United States by early morning, forming a line on the sidewalk that looped around the downtown extraction center that was close to the border crossing. At that particular place, maybe too close to the border guards' view to make an open interview comfortable, I couldn't find plasma sellers who wanted to speak with me. The sellers were more willing to chat in that strip-mall parking lot a few miles away. It was clear, though, from the long lines downtown and the busy parking lots elsewhere, that the trade was brisk and both sides of the business were making money on plasma.

In March that same year, when the United States closed the land border at the initial height of the pandemic, it knotted up finances for Gabriel and thousands of others who lived in Mexico's border towns and crossed into the U.S. The merit of closing a land border but not the air boundary never made much sense, but it was an easy way for the U.S. Border Patrol to ramp up hostility toward Mexican citizens who crossed over for any number of reasons—to see family, to go to college, to shop. This illogical partial closure came during the Trump years, amid the president's rantings about building a border wall and his bigoted tropes about Mexicans. But the bigger blow happened later.

In the United States, selling plasma is usually an income supplement. For Mexican citizens, it can be an entire income. The difference in what blood money means to people on either side of the border is vast. While plasma payments are relatively low in the context of U.S. average incomes, they can be a big deal for a Mexican family. Nobody knows this better than the international companies that harvest blood plasma along the border. In later court filings, they would say that 52 border blood plasma centers, out of more than 1,000 nationwide, produced an outsized 5 to 10 percent of the entire plasma pool collected in the United States.

During the border closure, Gabriel's stepfather passed away and his family was left struggling for money. He described those turbulent months as very challenging times. When the border reopened, Gabriel prepared to return, crossing over to have a vein tapped at the clinic and sell his plasma. But at his first visit back to the plasma center, he was informed by the staff that Mexican nationals visiting the United States on tourist visas would no longer be allowed to sell their blood plasma in El Paso, or anywhere else in this country. He and thousands of others had been caught up in an international legal fight over the blood of Mexican citizens. A market of daily blood immigrants had been cultivated for years unchecked as the industry built up extraction centers all along the frontier so they could mine Mexican blood for U.S. interests and global exports. For now, the practice was over.

Selling Plasma as Labor

In a press release in June 2021, the U.S. border patrol agency abruptly announced that it now considered crossing into this country to sell plasma to be "labor," something not allowed on day visits without a work visa. "Selling plasma constitutes labor for hire in violation of B-1 non-immigrant status, as both the labor (the taking of the plasma) and the accrual of profits would occur in the U.S.," the agency declared.

Several of the world's largest biomedical companies, including the U.S.-based subsidiaries of biomedicine giants CSL of Australia and Grifols of Spain, sued the U.S. Customs and Border Protection agency in 2022 over its policy change. They challenged the Border Patrol's pronouncement that selling plasma constituted labor, and in detail outlined how the long-established practice had drawn an estimated 10,000 Mexicans to cross the border every week for money, thereby fueling much of the global plasma supply. In their lawsuit, the companies said their borderland plasma extraction centers were the most productive in the country. Of more than 1,000 plasma centers across the United States, they said, the 52 set on the border were critical to their supply. For these massive companies, it was a blow both to the supply chain and to their bottom lines. They said it also posed a threat to people like me.

The companies argued that this sudden reversal of the thirty-

year-old practice of allowing donors to cross over without a work per-
mit inflicted harm on their business and on 125,000 patients in the
United States. Donating plasma, they said, is not labor. In fact, they
argued, the plasma pool is a sector of the United States economy so
important that it was declared a matter of national security in a different case. Interestingly, the companies also noted that other branches
of the federal government saw the issue differently and accepted the
practice as a service arrangement rather than work for hire.

"Crossing the border for a short period of time to donate plasma
is a paradigmatic example of 'visiting the United States temporarily
for business,'" they argued. "The vast majority of Mexican national
plasma donors cross the border into the U.S. to visit the plasma collection center, spend about 90 minutes there donating plasma after
their initial visit, receive a payment, perhaps buy a few items in the
U.S. (or not), and then return to Mexico the same day."

The filing described how the borderland plasma centers are the
most fruitful, accounting for an oversized share of all plasma donations in the United States. With a portion of the U.S. plasma pool ex-
ported to other countries for medications, an entire global operation
was put at risk by classifying the practice as labor. Few places in the
United States reveal inequality like the lands along the U.S.-Mexico
border, making it hard to imagine where companies like CSL and
Grifols might focus next if they were to make good on a threat to
move operations elsewhere.

The lawsuit also detailed the data on who owns what in the
American blood plasma economy, illustrating how an entire global
machine runs on the raw materials of American extraction. CSL
Plasma, a U.S. subsidiary of Australian biomedical giant CSL, has
about 290 plasma centers within the United States. The subsidiaries
of Grifols of Spain operate hundreds of centers. Each of the more
than 1,000 centers cost an estimated $2.5 million to build and em-
ploys at least 60 people, the filing said. Smaller companies make up
the rest of the numbers.

It wasn't just companies that would be hurt, they argued. "The
Plasma Ban will needlessly damage public health by making fewer
plasma-derived therapies available to patients at an inopportune
time," the companies claimed.

There is an obvious contradiction here. If one agency of the U.S.

government believes that Mexican nationals crossing over the border to sell plasma amounts to day labor, why then are millions of others who sell their plasma within the United States considered donors, not workers? The industry has more than tripled in its physical presence since 2005, all while insisting the payments for plasma are tokens of appreciation for people's time, not their labor. The federal government has not intervened in this arrangement anywhere but at the Mexico border.

———

The ban on crossing the border to sell plasma seemed to break a spell for many. Mexican citizens who had come to U.S. plasma centers in years past seemed to think a little harder about the long waits, hassles at the crossings, and middling pay. With that in the rearview mirror, some people's perspectives on the whole affair seemed to shift and they weren't interested in coming back. That's not to say new donors, perhaps younger, wouldn't fill the gap if the practice reopens to them.

The border rules left some stuck looking for low-paying work to fill the financial gap. For patients like me, it has perhaps meant higher prices as consumers. Indeed, the cost of my own medication rose about 30 percent during the pandemic, likely due to shortages in part created by the U.S.-Mexico border clampdown. That's never been stated outright—my medical bills and the price of plasma products remain concealed, in the same black box of proprietary information and illogical pricing that makes all the country's for-profit health care an infuriating mess.

If the United States is the OPEC of blood plasma, its pricing strategies do parallel those of the global oil cartel. Mexican citizens were paid an estimated $50 per donation to draw them over the border and into the plasma extraction centers of the United States, with the resource sold around the world. The proposition was less attractive to Americans than to people who earned lower incomes in another country.

———

Two massive biomedical companies based outside the United States are today the owners of much of the blood extraction economy in the U.S. Their collection stations represent some of the most prominent plasma brands in America. When I explain the paid-plasma donation system to friends in countries with good health-care systems and bans on payment for plasma extraction, I often get a response of "We don't allow that here." This is a global industry that targets disparity only where it can, and that translates to a bull's-eye painted firmly on the border with Mexico.

For years, plasma extracted in the United States from Mexicans who crossed the border helped feed the world's need for plasma. Their blood protein didn't just stay in the United States; it went around the globe and created profit in multiple countries. Wending my way through the complicated web of what is the global blood-plasma business, I began to understand that this is not a practice confined to the borders of a single country and run on cutthroat capitalism; it is an industry that exploits the United States' lack of protections for the poor and the working class, in the service of global medicine and profit.

Mexican citizens did not cross the border to sell plasma because they enjoyed it or carried a special desire to help people like me who need it. They did it because they needed the money. The companies figured out just how much would draw them in the door and set the payments accordingly, then drew a line at raising them much higher to lure in Americans who also lived along the border.

This was not only a local border war over blood but a global battle. Like most of the rest of the world, Mexico does not allow payment in exchange for plasma donations. Mexican donors cannot get paid for their plasma in their own country.

According to the Plasma Protein Therapeutics Association (PPTA), an industry organization, plasma donations were down by 20 percent in 2020, primarily due to the pandemic, and another 11 percent in 2021. The situation worsened, blood plasma companies said, when U.S. Customs and Border Protection changed its policy in 2021. The demand was going up, the industry said, while donations plummeted.

In May 2022, the U.S. Court of Appeals for the District of Columbia ruled in favor of the plasma companies, saying they had a legal right to challenge the Border Patrol's assertion that selling plasma constituted labor. Another ruling later in the year allowed Mexican nationals to resume selling plasma in the U.S. The legal fight over this thirty-year-old practice would continue.

A shift in El Paso's blood extraction centers was visible when I visited in 2021; those lines of donors that once snaked along the sidewalk at the downtown center where Gabriel and others used to sell their plasma were nonexistent eighteen months later. Although plasma companies insist that they do not prey on poorer communities, their reliance on blood from these collection centers at the border puts this claim to the test. The plasma industry also insists its blood comes from altruistic donors primarily invested in public service, yet its collection points in America inundate neighborhoods of Black and brown people, with few centers to be found in wealthy white enclaves.

In its Member Code of Ethics, the PPTA says its members will "select donors to obtain high quality source plasma while avoiding harmful and/or exploitative treatment of those donors."

Rethinking the Trade

A man I'll call Mateo, a 35-year-old former blood seller from Juárez, typifies perhaps why we don't see plasma centers spotting America's upper-middle-class suburbs. A lot of people he knew back home were selling their plasma; those who took part did well—coming back across the border with a nice extra helping of money for their time. For him, starting as an 18-year-old, his blood money went to buying concert tickets, taking vacations, and having drinks with his friends. He crossed over twice a week during summer and winter breaks from school, trekking across the bridge and down to the plasma station, where he would sit in a comfortable chair for forty minutes to an hour while the machine drew blood from his arm, separated out the plasma, and returned his red blood cells through the plastic tube inserted into his vein. At the time, it seemed like easy money.

Later, Mateo viewed the situation a little differently. He no longer saw it as something you should do long term or make a living of. He explained that taking an essential fluid out of your body might cause harm. He didn't have scientific proof, but that's what he felt.

Even though the practice of plasma collection is presented as entirely safe, with no potential future problems, and if you can pass basic health checks you can basically sell plasma forever, there is something about this system that just does not feel right. That's certainly true for many of the people who sell their plasma. Maybe it's the large loss of fluid, the repeated needle sticks, the injection of that anticlotting drug. Or maybe it's just the idea of giving up so much of your bodily fluids. And that crushing fatigue has been a real factor for so many donors I've met and spoken with. I can think of nothing so debilitating when done time and again that leaves behind no trace of harm. Like so many who used to at least know they had the option of making some extra money, Mateo heard about the new ban on plasma donations from Mexican citizens on day passes in the United States, exchanging a bodily resource for a small bit of security in tough times. But in a place like Juárez, the line between distressed and secure moves a little closer to the former than one might expect when living in better-off parts of the United States.

A woman in Juárez whom I'll call Sofia began selling plasma in her twenties while enrolled in college. Textbooks and other educational supplies added up to a few hundred dollars in her first semester that she didn't have. She described how it was common among her fellow dentistry students from Juárez to defray their costs with trips to El Paso's plasma centers. Full-time classes ruled out holding a regular job during the day, so steady appointments with the donor's chair fit well for people who didn't get sick at the idea or the process.

As a working single mother and student, Sofia lived somewhere in the middle. She began doing the plasma donations on the advice of friends and her sister—at first, she said, she thought the "saving lives" part was some weird new scam, a way to trick people out of something. But after donating a couple of times, she found the real problem was that it made her feel weak and dehydrated. Not the economic milieu or a bright-line example of inequity tangled up with race, but the literal process of selling blood. It took a total of about five hours to cross the border, wait in line, get stuck, and have her plasma extracted. She felt wrung out afterwards.

As a dental student, Sofia was more aware of the potential benefits of her gift and was fascinated by the idea that her plasma might go to someone in serious need. Maybe someone like me. She had learned about drugs like mine, and the plasma-derived blood-clotting agents used by hemophiliacs. It was meaningful for Sofia in ways others didn't seem to share. Even though she was donating plasma primarily to get paid, she was still doing her part for society.

It was an undertaking that benefited not just her, but also patients like me. Sofia said that she thought there are some bad ways to make money, but that this was something good.

When she thought about going back to the plasma center in El Paso to make some extra money after the border reopened, she found she could not, given the new rule that classified selling plasma as labor. While these companies depended on the blood and generosity of people who lived in Mexico, almost none of their public-relations goodwill in the legal case seemed aimed at serving the plasma donors. It's all about recipients, like me—people who pay a whole lot of money to access the medicines they produce. Curiously, I've never heard from a plasma company about how the border affects what my insurance company pays for the medication. I've not been told that my drug is in short supply. The companies' appeal rests on leveraging people like me to construct an argument. Knowing this, I began looking for better ways, for a clue as to how the system could be fairer for all of us. That led me to the brief, nearly forgotten moment in history when blood sellers formed a labor union.

CHAPTER 15
The Blood Givers' Union

*The American Federation of Labor granted a charter yesterday
to a union of professional blood donors on a promise that
the union's members would refrain from strikes.*
—New York Times, 1938

Diving into the world of paid-plasma extraction, into the country's giant pool of blood, has at times left me feeling like there's no hope for a better system. The plasma economy fueled by Americans and operated by global drug companies is too big, too secretive, too profitable, and too expertly targeted to the working class and poor—the members of our society who consistently get less attention, care, and assistance from our cultural and political spheres. But there is some hope to be found in looking back at history—specifically the 1930s in New York City.

Legions of American blood sellers did band together once to push back in a collective way, when they were a much smaller bloc of people earning money in a new industry. They organized their efforts in a manner that would culminate in a recognized labor union in 1938. It began in 1929, when New York City's top doctors and surgeons founded the Blood Transfusion Betterment Association and its Blood Donor Bureau, with a grant from John D. Rockefeller Jr. The organization started with the goals of supplying "the hospitals and physicians of New York City and, as far as practicable, the surrounding districts of New York State and New Jersey, with properly tested blood donors at any time of day or night with a minimum of delay," according to a 1930 explanation in the *Bulletin of the New York Academy of Medicine*.

In addition to outlining safe transfusion practices for both patients and blood donors, the association established payment schedules for blood donors. As a safety net, blood donors who showed up at the hospital on demand to offer a transfusion but were not needed by no fault of their own would be paid $2.50. That last item is more than the nothing plasma donors get when they are rejected from donating today, also through no fault of their own. But the rates set by the Association carved some money off the top and reduced the actual amount that went to the donors themselves. The donors, unhappy with their pay cut and limits on how often they could sell blood, unionized.

The blood donors' collective of New York, and the later Blood Givers' Union, was formed not long before Charles Drew's big innovation led to the creation of the country's first blood banks, a revolution in modern science that allowed medical facilities to store blood for future use rather than relying on direct transfusion. But before the blood banks, donors were badly needed, with regularity and immediacy, because transfusion was a patient-to-patient process; they had to be ready to donate on demand and at hospitals.

With the invention and mainstreaming of lifesaving transfusions came the blood drives, and ongoing searches for people who would accept money in exchange for their blood. This was whole blood, not plasma, and the people who sold it recognized its worth at a time also marked by labor union mobilization across the country. Within just a few years of massing into a united labor force, the blood sellers, who earned a part or all of their income from offering up veins for the extraction of their blood, recognized that physical labor and body parts held value and they deserved a fair wage for allowing science and medicine to use their blood. They organized into a workers' union that became a member of the American Federation of Labor (AFL), then one of the largest umbrella union groups in the country. The blood givers' union didn't last long, but that's likely because advances in blood banking made their services much less urgently needed.

The country's medical systems still needed blood at that time, but donors no longer had to be available right on the spot. The scientific advance likely scuttled the pressing demand for a labor union of blood sellers. In 1938, the *New York Times* wrote about the union in a somewhat humorous tone, interviewing a union leader about the particulars of what members expected to be paid for transfusion work. The paper joked about the AFL's rivalry with its competing union, citing the blood givers' rep: "He did not disclose what might happen if an A.F. of L. donor met a C. of I. O. [Congress of Industrial Organizations] patient, but he emphasized that his organization would always be guided by 'the best interests of society.'"

The blood givers' union of New York, representing 150 members, established accepted rates for the time required in the extraction of their blood. They also made some key concessions for the benefit of blood buyers and society at large. It all seems perfectly reasonable, although the newspaper account appears to make light of the union. In 1938, when the union was granted its AFL chapter, professional blood sellers would be paid between $7 and $10 per 100 cubic centimeters of blood, a healthy amount of money for a one-hour endeavor almost a century ago. In return for their wage guarantee, they agreed to refrain from striking and to offer free blood donations if the blood was being used to treat the indigent. A primary goal of the blood sellers' union was to standardize payments to blood donors. But blood bureaus pushed back against the union, calling donation of blood a purely altruistic act that was compensated only for the time spent. It was not, they insisted, an act of labor compensated with wages.

The short-lived union drive seems relevant to the plasma industry today. Though the blood givers' union faded out as the United States entered World War II, a collective group establishing minimum rates for their body parts seems like common sense today. The Second World War changed the blood industry in every way, including the development of plasma—a much more useful, storable, and transferrable material than whole blood. Whole blood sellers weren't in such immediate demand. I wasn't able to find a mention of the blood union movement beyond New York or past that first year of its existence; it appears to have been more of a local movement made obsolete by science. Still, I can't help but think how badly such a union is needed today. If the millions of plasma sellers in America were unionized, they might be able to build power beyond the opaque pay scale. If we recognized that giving up one's plasma twice a week is *labor*, rather than a wholly altruistic endeavor, the companies extracting it might be compelled to compensate for it more fairly.

———

While the practice of paying people for donating whole blood is banned in the United States, the plasma industry parrots the language that was used against the New York blood sellers' union in the 1930s. Donating plasma is an altruistic act, they insist, and donors are compensated only for their time, not their labor. They say this is not a work-for-pay arrangement. But my survey of plasma sellers undercuts this argument.

In that informal online poll I conducted of more than forty people who have sold their plasma and wanted to elaborate on their reasons, every respondent said they did it primarily for the money. Knowing that it served those in need was a happy side benefit, but it was never the main reason that drew them to begin selling plasma. It is difficult to believe an argument that selling blood plasma is not labor when nearly everyone I've spoken with tells me they engage in the practice because it pays. Yet the plasma industry promotes this idea, with one difference.

Today, as in the 1930s, whole blood is primarily drawn and traded by nonprofit organizations. The plasma trade is mostly run by massive profit-making corporations—companies that don't often reveal their inner workings. I had to go undercover at the Flint plasma center to discover how the process works; the staff wasn't supposed to show journalists around. As this is a business centered on making profits, and not a charity, any additional scrutiny is a potential liability.

As employment—and just about everything else—has become more exploitative in America, unions have once again gained in popularity. Support for labor unions has grown from 55 percent across the country in the late 1990s to 71 percent by 2022, marking the widest growth in public support since 1965, according to polling from Gallup. The sheer numbers don't yet reflect this shift, but unions are especially popular with today's younger workers. In fact, recent years have seen massive organizing efforts at facilities of major businesses like Starbucks, REI, and even Amazon, which saw its first warehouse unionization in Staten Island, New York, in March 2022.

This modern era of renewed interest in union organizing harkens back to those first decades of the twentieth century, when even the people who donated blood could draw themselves together into a labor movement. Union membership in the United States peaked in 1954, when 35 percent of the workforce was in one or another union; by 1983, that percentage had plummeted to 20 percent, and was down to 10 percent of the workforce by 2020. Now that blood plasma sellers number in the millions, I'm wondering if a blood sellers' union could be viable again. There are so many more people now selling their plasma, and collective action could improve the situation for them. Specifically, the implementation of a plasma minimum wage could make this entire endeavor fairer for the people on whom it depends. Maybe unionization would provide a layer of self-regulation, especially in terms of the number of times people could donate in a week or month, and for how long.

Studies have shown that workers in unionized workplaces are more likely to speak out about health and safety problems, knowing that their union will have their back. With that support system, why wouldn't it make sense for these blood sellers to have similar protections and rights? It's difficult to make the case that the sliding scale of payments designed to keep donors coming back as often as possible does not equate to an employment policy.

I've spent so many years now digging into the stories around selling blood. I have found a country out of alignment with the promises of its reputation. Mass economic precarity, callous corporate power brokers, a voiceless underclass hooked up to be milked for their blood plasma. In the end, it was hard for me not to land on one solution that seemed to have worked the last time we were so wracked by inequality: the union. Or at least some kind of acknowledgment that the people who sell plasma are engaging in something akin to labor and should be compensated fairly and protected for it.

CHAPTER 16
What to Do About the Giant Pool

You can save lives while
earning some money!
—CSL Plasma

In the fifteen or so years that I lived in China, I was fascinated by the dystopian tales of that country's plasma economy. Even the name seemed too strange for it to have been a reality. It was real, of course. The idea and the result of constructing a moneymaking scheme around the extraction and sale of the blood of poor people, or even of people just living on the economic fringes, seemed right out of a science fiction novel, one that at many turns was hardly believable. Back then, I thought it was a plan so brazenly weird that only China in that era would attempt to pull it off. It seemed to me a gross manifestation of unchecked greed to leech a lifegiving substance from people who need money so it could be sold by some faceless entity to make profits for a higher authority.

I traveled through Henan and nearby provinces extensively in those years, writing stories for newspapers and magazines about the consequences of the scheme, the blood-borne AIDS epidemic, the ongoing deaths and protests, and the heavy-handed cover-ups. That country's haphazard, rushed attempt to create a massive domestic blood plasma industry, sped along by greed, became instead a model for how not to handle a public health crisis. By placing profits ahead of safety and by cutting corners, China's plasma system infected hundreds of thousands of Chinese people with HIV, and its true impact remains concealed to this day.

The farmers of Henan sold their blood plasma at a frenzied pace, and when HIV entered the corrupted system, as many as a million people were infected. By the time I met the whistleblowers Wang Shuping and Gao Yaojie in the United States, I had developed a smug conviction that our system here was much better, or at least a little kinder. There's a mental deception that happens when you live outside your own country for a long time, when you begin to idealize home and see past its faults. I naively never suspected that America's massive plasma pool, what I now know is a $24 billion-a-year global industry, was born almost entirely of the same idea—taking advantage of people who need money. I thought I would find at least a few people who sold plasma primarily for altruistic reasons. I did not meet one. In the course of investigating the practice and of interviewing more than 100 people who sell or have sold their plasma, I've begun to understand the truth about America and why this country, without much notice, has become the home of the real plasma economy. As the rich have grown richer, the non-rich have taken to selling their blood parts in ever-growing numbers.

Before she died in 2019, Wang Shuping led me to the doorway of seeing how things here are potentially just as bad as they were back in China, but in different ways. She knew somehow, just from getting a glimpse of the speed at which it was operating, that the American system was as predatory as the one she had exposed back in China. She also knew something was wrong, but she wasn't able to see yet exactly what that was, and she wanted me to find out more. Today, the plasma industry appears to be safe from viral infections like the kind that wiped out the practice in China, a cautionary tale that's been absorbed the world over. Wang Shuping didn't live long enough see the coronavirus spread like a brushfire through China and out into the world, sickening and killing millions of people. In our conversations, it was clear she understood from her own experiences that as long as heavy-handed governments continue to crush information vital to public safety, a terrible crisis could strike again.

It's not an exact parallel with what is happening to plasma sellers in America; few events pair so closely. And yet, the United States has built a dystopian sector similar to what China dreamed of creating. It consists of a network of hundreds of plasma extraction centers, deliberately built in economically disadvantaged neighborhoods, towns, and cities. Places like Flint, Michigan, and Rexburg, Idaho, and El Paso, Texas. Places where companies know people need money and might do something a little unpleasant to get it. The centers prey on the precarity of people who live in these places, often ignored by the wider public, and a little bit too dark to dive deep under the surface. They use an American mixture of cheery customer service and ever-changing payment schemes that can make plasma sellers feel like they are the ones gaming the system, when reality is the other way around. They draw in more people of color because they are often built in the places where most people aren't white. It is an industry that takes advantage of baked-in American economic and racial inequities.

The plasma industry has done all of this without too many people in power taking notice, in large part because the practice doesn't affect the lives of the comfortable among us. Unless you are sick like me, most middle-class and wealthier white people don't spend a lot of time thinking about the plasma centers they might pass on the road, who the people are who are selling their blood, or where all that blood comes from and goes. Until I dug under the surface, I didn't know either. It's easy, almost comforting, to believe it is a practice reserved for only the poorest, or people reliant on drugs or alcohol. In truth, many of the poorest and most downtrodden people are screened out of the system and prohibited from selling their plasma. They never even make it past the questionnaire that demands a permanent home address and basic blood work. America's wealth gap has grown so wide that teachers, journalists, and many other workers in what were, not so long ago, solidly middle-class professions have fallen into a shaky existence that compels them to sell pieces of their bodies to live more comfortably. Plasma sellers can be found just about everywhere, if you just ask around. The plasma industry knows this, and it relies upon that reality for its giant pool of yellowish liquid.

Even though we have millions of people in America who sell their blood plasma either as a temporary fix or for long-term income, we don't know what that does to their bodies. Absent robust, independent scientific studies, there are endless anecdotes: stories of fainting, of being too weak to work, of feeling like they're recovering from the flu. Medical science offers almost no data on the long-term effects of donorship but still we have collectively decided it's fine for people who are broke to sell their blood twice a week for as long as possible. For-profit companies present plasma donation as simply a way to make money and save lives in the process. These plasma sellers do change lives, like mine, but many times their own health is almost certainly affected, at least temporarily. A practice that makes some people faint and feel ill, or need to sleep for hours—done twice a week for years on end—can't be that innocuous. It deserves more study.

It's in the corporations' best interests to keep the science murky: if we knew more about the negative effects, perhaps pharmaceutical companies would have fewer donations to fill the giant pool of plasma. In the years I've been digging beneath the surface of plasma selling, I've grown more uneasy with each infusion I receive. The stories of plasma sellers and what brought them to this point linger in my mind.

In Idaho, it's college students and housewives who need extra income. In Michigan, it's people who live in places that created and sustained the American middle class, but that system has failed them and left their families to scramble for ways to make ends meet. In Texas, along the border, it's the citizens of a poorer nation who, for thirty years, fed America's giant pool of blood, the contents then dispersed here and across the world. All of this depends on a large, ongoing number of people needing extra income, on a system where even hard work doesn't pay enough to provide a decent living. We have a society where students take on massive debt and still need extra money. Where what were once middle-class jobs, like working as a teacher or a local news reporter, now don't pay enough to afford the basics like good housing, paying off little debts, and maybe having the chance to have some fun once in a while. I've met so many people who sell their blood plasma for so many different reasons. There is no one story. People who don't want or need the payments usually donate plasma or blood at the Red Cross, their local hospital, or through another nonprofit organization. Paid plasma extraction is, I have come to believe, low-paid, exploited labor. But we shy away from seeing it as such. The system is set up to lure people in with money, with its complicated schedule of payments and rewards determined by suits in offices somewhere far away, and that's exactly what it does. The answer to fixing things lies in recognizing it as labor, not strictly altruism.

Our most personal substance—the essential fluid believed to be the essence of life throughout human history—has become a commodity, a substance traded for profit at the expense of the most vulnerable, the people who have few other choices. When I launched into this investigation, I expected to come away with some wonky ideas about how to fix a small industry that affected a few hundred thousand people in the United States. What I found instead is millions of people selling their plasma, and a hungry machine, rich and growing richer, that goes about its business of making medicine, researching, and earning profits quietly. The fundamental problem with the plasma business lies not in the practices of drawing people's plasma but in the flaws inherent in American capitalism. We have begun to accept that people can and should do whatever it takes to get by—as the rich get even richer, it's fine for teachers and truck drivers to sell their blood to make ends meet.

———

I am thinking about all this and writing as a bag of plasma-borne medicine drips into the tube that snakes to a vein on the back of my left hand. Infusion days, the boring hours sitting in that red recliner chair, are often when I think about the industry the most. Mostly I marvel at how many people it lures in, how much plasma it draws out, and how little notice most people have taken that it is a crutch within the American economy. Selfishly, I wonder whether revealing all this will affect my own health. Will people stop donating plasma if they know just how predatory the business can be? Will the price of my own medication go up if fewer people sell their plasma? Most people have agency over their bodies in this regard; they are not forced or compelled by a higher hand to sell their plasma, unlike the prison schemes of the 1980s in Arkansas. It's money that pressures them to donate, I know. I've now met so many people who've done it and didn't feel they had better choices, it's clear to me it's not a fun way to pass the time, or what most people would do twice a week if given a choice. Many have told me they would do it, once in a while, to help out, even if it didn't pay. But occasional donations don't sate the world's demand for human plasma.

From talking with experts and academics who study the industry, I began to understand how a few small changes could make the practice better for now. A plasma minimum wage, clearly outlined and fairly paid, would provide transparency and give donors more choice about how often they give. And more scientific research is needed to determine whether frequent, long-term plasma donation—the kind the industry encourages—is actually safe. If it is, why are we the only country in the world that allows people to donate twice a week for years on end?

Beyond that, what would give plasma sellers more freedom of choice is fixing American capitalism and repairing the broken social safety net. Raising the federal minimum wage would make life fairer for everyone. So, too, would universal health care and completely wiping out student debt—medical and college debt are two heavy financial burdens I've heard several plasma donors say forced them to return to the practice more often than they would have liked. It's hard to think of a more obvious, blunt symbol of a broken economic system than people selling blood to pay for an education or pay down medical bills. Until we fix the underlying problems that make ours an increasingly unequal society, millions of people will be pressed to sell their blood plasma. And I will have no choice but to keep buying and using it.

EPILOGUE

How bizarre.
How bizarre, how bizarre.
—OMC

A twisted thing happens when you are a woman who gets sick in America. In the beginning, when something goes wrong with your body, there is very often an arduous road to being believed at all. You know what isn't working, you know how it feels and can describe it, but getting a doctor to take it seriously can be a whole other matter. It's a phenomenon that's been well documented and is more common, often manifesting in even more brutal ways for women who are not white. Even when the symptoms are severe and maybe deadly, the road to being believed can feel like climbing a mountain when your legs don't work. In my case, this all meant years of being turned away from multiple doctors' offices, told it was all in my head, even though I could barely walk or use my hands. Something was obviously, visibly wrong with me, but it took years to be believed by anyone who would treat me. Medical gaslighting is real. It betrays itself when medical professionals tell women we are fine, that nothing is wrong, that we need to stop being so hysterical. That's how it was for me.

It is a well-known enough phenomenon that women routinely share information about which doctors will listen and which ones to avoid. For me, a previously perfectly healthy 20-something when my body broke down in the 1990s, I didn't want to believe it was true. Taking the bad, condescending advice of all the male doctors who told me it was all in my head was somehow comforting. I did not want to believe there was anything truly wrong with my body, so I slipped into denial and stopped going to doctors until it became impossible to walk.

But when you do find out your body is not, in fact, working and you are sick, the atmosphere shifts again. There is an expectation in this society, especially for women, that getting sick causes a metamorphosis—a change that we like to believe leads to some sort of redemption. That illness causes us to find the true meaning in life, to slow down, to take more time with the people we love, to appreciate the small moments in life. None of this ever resonated with me. I was young, active, and busy when I got sick. I was also trying to make a living in a country that doesn't mandate paid sick leave, a place where discrimination against illness and disability is woven into the fabric of life. I did not feel blessed with some special knowledge about the meaning of life when I found out I was sick. I still don't feel it. As I write this, my hands are clumsy and prone to typos. I've had a major medical crash, and it will take a while for my limbs to start working properly. I am tired and cranky. There isn't much more to it.

Being sick has always been annoying, then and now, and it still makes me outwardly irritable when I think about it for too long. I can remember appreciating many of the small moments in life long before my hands and feet went numb; but this didn't make me more aware of them. Illness did not heighten my ability to see the greater good in people, but it did hone my perceptions of how unequal and punitive America's systems, including health care, are for people who aren't wealthy. America loves sick women who suffer in silence, but this society doesn't love people as much when they push back against systems that stigmatize illness and disability.

But I do want to know how we got to the point where illness came to be looked upon as a noble endeavor, even though it's a more messy, unpleasant, fraught existence. Until recently, the narrative of being sick in America was largely shaped by personal history, mostly relayed by middle-class or wealthy white women following a predictable arc of redemption at the end of which they find meaning in falling ill.

This is how we like to imagine sick people in America—quiet

and stoic. It's also how society would like people with chronic conditions to behave, because it better serves the interests of an economic system that demands perfect health and optimal productivity. Nowhere was that more evident than during a global pandemic, when federal and state governments pushed to end concerns about the virus before its dangers had passed, urging Americans back to work. Quietly weathering your ordeal, as though it's a solely personal concern, is preferable to speaking out about systemic injustices in medicine, in health care, in every facet of American life.

In 1999, Anne Hunsaker Hawkins, a professor of humanities at Pennsylvania State University, explored the question of illness memoirs in her book *Reconstructing Illness*. Hawkins found that personal accounts of illness began to proliferate in the United States in the 1950s; before then, the genre did not exist in great depth. The stories began to snowball into publications and popular culture. Hawkins found that in the mid-1990s there were sixty memoirs about breast cancer alone. These stories were and are read; they don't vanish into a vacuum. People connect with tales of bodies gone wrong. We all know illness and death will happen to us one day, but there is an appeal in reading someone else's account of pain and personal tragedy. These stories give us a glimpse into parts of our lives we don't often speak about with strangers, a peek into private tragedies and hardship. A novel but real life. I wouldn't exactly call it voyeurism, but there's a persistent element of that in the popularity of illness memoirs and movies. We like reading about and watching stories that delve into the darkness and pain lived by other people. Interrogating our own pain can be much more difficult.

In her book, Hawkins describes the illness memoir as a work that "offer[s] us a disquieting glimpse of what it is like to live in the absence of order and coherence." The authors stitch the pieces back together again. People enjoy the illness story, but for me it usually lacks what is fundamental: the financial cost of being sick in a country without universal health care and with the profit motive at the heart of the system.

For many years, I considered writing an illness memoir, probably because it seemed like the thing to do when you are writer and live with a serious illness. There is a lot to think about, but what is there to say about this illness that hasn't been said? My limbs go numb, then they come back to life. Over and over and over again. It probably won't kill me, but then again, maybe it will. Nobody knows why it happens. One aspect of having an incredibly rare illness is how it provokes a tendency to look for others similarly afflicted. There are few people who have what I have, and the famous ones are all men. For whatever reason, the disease appears to be more common in men than in women, more prevalent in older people than in younger. So, from the time I was in my twenties, I've been reading illness stories about men who were decades older than I was. The truth of their illnesses often emerged when they died, which made me question whether what I have is as innocuous and manageable as I like to tell myself. I've never had a doctor say this disease might kill me. Each medical interaction has been focused on managing the present, controlling the symptoms, and looking for possible progression of the disease. Every so often, I run down the list of high-profile people who have or had it, especially the few I know who have died from it.

There was Indiana senator Richard Lugar, an 87-year-old staple of twentieth-century American politics who died in 2019. According to a Lugar Center statement, "the cause of death was complications from CIDP (chronic inflammatory demyelinating polyneuropathy)." He lived more years than the average American's life expectancy, so I was more interested in learning how he kept it hidden for his entire political career than I was in knowing he died at age 87. I knew his name but not much else about him.

There are others, some with stories that are a little more frightening. I think I have read them all, and they are always obscure. People I wouldn't have paid much attention to if we didn't have this shared connection. Do you remember the band Otara Millionaires Club? They had that one big hit song in the 1990s, "How Bizarre," an earworm of the highest order. The song plays once in a while on local radio, and whenever I hear it, I become that person with a little factoid stuck in my head that I'll probably need to share with you. Lead singer Paul Fuemana died at age 40 in New Zealand of complications from CIDP. Obsessive reading about Fuemana told me the exact cause of death was respiratory failure after a "protracted battle" with the same disease I have. I've never been warned this is a possibility.

When Fuemana died in 2010, the New Zealand media reported that his illness was fatal in 10 percent of cases. One news story described it as "something of a medical mystery." It sounds like a cop-out, but no, it's true. The 10 percent fatality rate is a statistic I often find floating around in places like Wikipedia, online news stories, and other sources that don't link directly to hard scientific data. Is it accurate? Two decades into this life, I honestly have no idea. My best guess is that with underlying factors, and without access to good treatment options, the disease can be a lot more dangerous. Fuemana was never properly diagnosed and treated, as far as I can tell. I asked one of my doctors once if the illness is deadly in 10 percent of cases, and the answer was cloudier than the question: "We really don't know." Rare conditions, lesser understood, come with a lot of professional shrugging.

And then there was Joseph Heller, who for a long time was the only fairly famous person I'd heard of who had my disease. The author of *Catch-22* even wrote a little book about being sick, called *No Laughing Matter*. Okay, but wait; Heller had Guillain-Barré syndrome, a much more common and severe variation of my illness—and the book is more of a humorous celebration of friendship than an illness memoir. He spent his sick time cracking jokes and eating Chinese food with his friends. It was a fun read, from an entirely different time, but again, not the slightest bit relatable for me. I always look for the cause of death in cases like these, and I was a bit relieved to find that Heller died of a heart attack, not complications from his condition.

The stories are few and scattered; there is no real clear prognosis, but it doesn't seem all that bad. Instead of finding the answer, I have read dozens and dozens of illness memoirs over the years, looking for shared truths about being sick with a condition that most people don't understand. Reading about the complicated lives of others can somehow help make sense of your own, even in bits and pieces.

In many books and essays, I've found some I can relate to. But I'm almost always relating to fragmented symptoms or to the solitary parts of being sick. In many popular depictions of illness, I've found an empty space where I want to know how patients can afford to get sick in America. But none of this is shocking. Those without wealth don't often have their voices heard in stories that go viral. I think the people who sell their plasma—the substance that ends up treating my strange illness—are a lot more interesting than the mundane annoyance of my feet going numb. But I now understand how it all connects.

This book began as a quest to find the people on whose plasma I depend as a perpetual living vampire. I wanted to understand the people on whose generosity I rely. I expected to come away with some ideas about how to make the system better for a small group of marginalized Americans who sell their blood plasma. Maybe some specific plans drawn from health studies or the work of scientists, some ideas about health impacts. Instead, I found a splintered society divided by economics. Millions of people sell their blood parts every year, and it's nearly always a matter of bettering their financial circumstances.

The answer does not lie in a scientific study. The practice itself is not obscure. It is common, widespread, and propelled by the vast and growing chasm of economic imbalances that grip this country. My journey morphed into something else: an exploration of the inequality that forces millions of people to sell their blood while others look away. At the beginning of this endeavor, when I was looking for plasma sellers, I fell into a bottomless well of stories about American life for those who aren't rich. What happens when jobs that used to provide a middle-class living—teaching, TV journalism, making cars—no longer pay enough to keep up with basic bills and some extra fun on the side?

I knew my medicine did not come cheap. What I've spent out of my own pocket has added up to at least $100,000 over some twenty years that could have been spent on a down payment for a home, building retirement savings, or on so many other items that add up to a normal, stable life. And yet, after talking with more than 100 people who sell their plasma to get by, I know I'm luckier than a whole lot of others in my situation. For years, on the other side of the world, I protected myself by smuggling blood. I believed China's system, a protected tangle of corruption that allowed the blood supplies to remain at risk, was a problem I could navigate. I didn't know then that the plasma economy in my own country, fertilized by cutthroat capitalism and exploitation, was burgeoning unchecked and mostly ignored. The exploitation from which my medicine is derived, the giant pool of plasma refilled each day by people on the ropes, favors me—for now.

ACKNOWLEDGMENTS

This book would not have been possible without many people, first and foremost the plasma sellers across the United States and in Mexico who shared their stories with me, and whose vital fluids keep me upright and moving through life.

For my reporting about China, Drs. Wang Shuping and Gao Yaojie were instrumental in unearthing and publicizing the story of what happened there. Both women were more than generous with their time and encouragement. Also, thanks to Wan Yanhai and Xi Chen for their documentation of selling plasma in China and its impacts. Ruby Yang's documentary on AIDS in China and the writing of Yan Lianke, who was quite generous with his time on more than one occasion, are some of the blocks on which this work was built. Maple Chen helped translate interviews in the United States. Several colleagues who still live in China and can't be named, for their safety, assisted with research and translation. Sharron Lovell, the best travel and reporting partner in the world, helped make sometimes dicey research trips through China fun and fruitful, and she encouraged this work for years.

In Rexburg, Idaho, Rett Nelson helped me better understand the place. I'm deeply grateful to Meg Conley for sharing her knowledge of the altruistic aspects and history of the Mormon Church. In Flint, Michigan, journalists Scott Atkinson and Jacob Carah helped me better grasp the city, its past, and its importance in American labor.

In El Paso, I'm deeply indebted to journalist Verónica Martínez for finding the people I interviewed at length, and for making connections and calls. Thanks also to Mónica Ortiz Uribe and Elliott Woods for connecting me to people. Darryl Lorenzo Wellington was especially generous with his experience, walking me through the process of plasma selling and some of the more ludicrous aspects of the game. Nate Monroe in Florida helped find a missing puzzle piece in court documents.

At the University of Michigan, poverty expert Luke Shaefer guided me through the numbers of plasma sellers and helped me realize there are many more than I suspected. Adam T. Perzynski, at Case Western Reserve University in Ohio, explained how the plasma industry geotargets communities. There are others who helped with that but can't be named.

In Tokyo, a fellowship from the Japan Center for International Exchange allowed me to spend time with people who had been infected with HIV, and I'm grateful to Ryuhei Kawada for his time and sharing his story.

My agent, Ian Bonaparte, saw the value in this book and helped shape it into what it is now. My editor, Nicholas Ciani, took a chance on this work and supported me throughout, helping me mold the book into what it needed to become. Nick's edits made the writing shine. To both of them, I'm forever indebted. Hannah Murphy Winter, the world's best and kindest fact-checker, made all the reporting stronger, and she did it fast. Thanks to One Signal Publishing for taking on this project.

Friends and colleagues Jocelyn Ford, Dustin Knievel, Donald Pacheco, Rachael Buchanan, Marsha Cooke, Christina Boutrup, Stephanie Kleine-Ahlbrandt, Samantha Culp, Anne Helen Petersen, Joe Kolman, Ericka Schenck, Antonia Malchik, and so many others provided support, encouragement, and threads of help throughout. Thanks to Gwen Lockman for reading an early draft (in one day!) and Mary Kay Magistad for her invaluable edits.

This book would not exist without the insistent prodding of Louisa Lim. Thanks to Jessica Reed for publishing the first piece of this thread in the *Guardian* and to the Banff Centre for Arts and Creativity, where a generous writing residency guided by Susan Orlean and Carol Shaben offered me invaluable time and feedback that made the writing much better. Thanks to Jon Lee Anderson and the editors of *Reportagen* magazine in Switzerland for cheering me on to write more about this topic. And thanks to Susan, also, for the name.

I'm especially grateful to my family for putting up with me during this process, especially Andrew, and to my sister, Beth, for reading an early version of the book. Any errors and omissions in this work are entirely my own.

NOTES

vii **blind to their suffering:** Gao Yaojie, interview with author, various times 2012–2014, New York.

PROLOGUE: Smuggling Blood

1 The Chinese government banned exactly this—imported blood: "China Bans Import of Blood Products to Keep AIDS Out," *Los Angeles Times*, September 3, 1985, https://www.la times.com/archives/la-xpm-1985-09-03-mn-24467-story.html

2 **China was still grabbling with an AIDS epidemic:** Elizabeth Rosenthal, "China Now Facing an AIDS Epidemic, Top Aid Admits," *New York Times*, August 24, 2001, https://www.ny times.com/2001/08/24/world/china-now-facing-an-aids-epi demic-a-top-aide-admits.html

2 **six global drug companies:** Walt Bogdanich and Eric Koll, "2 Paths of Bayer Drug in 80's: Riskier One Steered Overseas," *New York Times*, May 22, 2003, https://www.nytimes .com/2003/05/22/business/2-paths-of-bayer-drug-in-80-s -riskier-one-steered-overseas.html. The six companies were Baxter, Armour Pharmaceuticals, Bayer, Alpha Therapeutic, Aventis Behring, and Aventis; see Andrew L. Wang, "Baxter Suing Insurer to Recoup Millions in Bad Blood Settlements," *Crain's Chicago Business*, January 24, 2012, https://www

.chicagobusiness.com/article/20120124/NEWS03/120129907
/baxter-suing-insurer-to-recoup-millions-in-bad-blood-settle
ments

2   **Thousands of hemophiliacs around the world:** Andrew Pol-
lack, "Dying of AIDS, Japanese Youth Wants Apology," *New York
Times*, October 29, 1995, https://archive.nytimes.com/www.ny
times.com/library/national/science/aids/102995sci-aids.html.
Also, Kathleen McLaughlin, "The AIDS Granny in Exile," *Buzz-
Feed*, December 1, 2012, https://www.buzzfeed.com/kathleen
mclaughlin/the-aids-granny-in-exile

3   **keep the disease from filtering:** *The Blood of Yingzhou District*, film directed by Ruby Yang, produced by Thomas Lennon,
China AIDS Media Project, 2006.

3   **Thousands unwittingly took the disease home:** Gao Yaojie, T*he
Soul of Gao Yaojie* (Hong Kong: Ming Pao Publications, 2017).

3   **spread by China's domestic trade in human blood plasma:**
Elizabeth Rosenthal, "In Rural China, a Steep Price of Poverty:
Dying of AIDS," *New York Times*, October 28, 2000, https://
www.nytimes.com/2000/10/28/world/in-rural-china-a-steep
-price-of-poverty-dying-of-aids.html

3   **stories of HIV and hepatitis infections carried through commercial blood:** Dylan Sutherland and Jennifer Hsu, *HIV/AIDS
in China—The Economic and Social Determinants* (London:
Routledge, 2011).

5   **Charlene Barshefsky, was busted:** Annie Groer and Ann
Gerhart, "Beijing Beanie Baby Bonanza," *Washington Post*,
July 3, 1998, https://www.washingtonpost.com/archive/life
style/1998/07/03/the-reliable-source/c78621f4-2222-44d9
-a97b-1cc3d8c75017/

6   **entire villages began mobilizing around:** "Bleak Times in
Bra Town," *Economist*, April 16, 2016, https://www.economist
.com/china/2016/04/16/bleak-times-in-bra-town

7   **across the region in the mid-1990s:** Yan Lianke, interview with
author, 2014, Beijing.

7   **The grass upon the plain:** Yan Lianke, *Dream of Ding Village*,
translation by Cindy Carter (New York: Open Road/Grove/
Atlantic Press translation, 2011).

9   **roughly 1 million people were infected:** Shelley Torcetti, *Living*

in the Shadows of China's HIV/AIDS Epidemics: Sex, Drugs and Bad Blood (London: Routledge, 2021).

9   **Were it not for two women:** Gao, *Soul of Gao Yaojie.*

9   **AIDS had become the leading cause of death:** Z. Wu, J. Chen, S. R. Scott, and J. M. McGoogan, "History of the HIV Epidemic in China," *Current HIV/AIDS Reports* 16, no. 6 (2019): 458–66, https://doi.org/10.1007/s11904-019-00471-4

10 **perfect personality to publicly take on:** "Restrictions on AIDS Activists in China," Human Rights Watch, June 2005, https://www.hrw.org/reports/2005/china0605/china0605.pdf

12 **apart from one personal essay:** Wang Shuping, "How I Discovered the HIV Epidemic and What Happened to Me Afterwards," *China Change,* September 27, 2012.

CHAPTER 1: The Whistleblower

13 **outdoors, hiking the trails in the nearby mountains:** Wang Shuping, interviews with author and correspondence with author, 2017–2019, Salt Lake City.

17 **the clinics exposed healthy plasma sellers:** Anna Hayes, "AIDS, Bloodheads & Cover-Ups: The 'Abc' of Henan's Aids Epidemic," *Australian Quarterly* 77, no. 3 (2005): 12–40, http://www.jstor.org/stable/20638337

21 **something equally calamitous could happen here:** Arwa Mahdawi, "If the Poorest Americans Are Selling Their Blood, the US Is in Serious Trouble," *Guardian,* October 21, 2020, https://www.theguardian.com/commentisfree/2020/oct/21/if-the-poorest-americans-are-selling-their-blood-the-us-is-in-serious-trouble

21 ***The King of Hell's Palace:*** "Meet the Whistleblowing Heroine Who Inspired *The King of Hell's Palace:* Dr. Shuping Wang," Q&A at the Hampstead Theatre, August 29, 2019, https://www.hampsteadtheatre.com/news/2019/august/a-q-and-a-with-dr-shuping-wang/?fbclid=IwAR20M0BKZ-HggBlnjAgb0wvtjpoDbqH1NsCPc3hhMOd_sLuXhAE6-32jNLw

21 **Back in China:** Wang Shuping. Full statement on Chinese government pressure, September, 9, 2019, https://www.hampsteadtheatre.com/news/2019/september/full-statement-dr-shuping-wang/

22 **Two decades on:** Vanessa Thorpe, "From Beijing to Hampstead," *The Observer*, September 8, 2019, https://www.theguardian .com/stage/2019/sep/08/the-king-of-hells-palace-hampstead -theatre-shuping-wang-hiv-whistleblower-china

22 **I am in America now:** Dr. Wang Shuping, statement released by the Hampstead Theatre, London. https://www.hampsteadthe atre.com/news/2019/september/full-statement-dr-shuping -wang/

22 **Within weeks, she was gone:** Obituary for Wang Shuping, *Salt Lake Tribune*, September 2019, https://www.legacy.com /us/obituaries/saltlaketribune/name/shuping-wang-obituary ?id=2080695

24 **On that promise, I set out:** "America's Booming Blood Plasma Industry," *Economist*, May 10, 2018, https://www.economist .com/international/2018/05/10/americas-booming-blood -plasma-industry

CHAPTER 2: The Sellers

25 **The clinic, tucked into the development:** Derek Gilliam, "Boyfriend: Truck Pushed Woman's Car into Jacksonville Plasma Donation Center," *Florida Times-Union*, October 27, 2014, https://www.jacksonville.com/story/news/crime/2014/10/27 /boyfriend-woman-accused-plasma-center-crash-says-truck -pushed-car/15785856007/

25 **Inside the waiting room:** Case files, arrest and booking reports, Clerk of the Circuit Court, Duvall County, Florida, 2014.

26 **The woman returned to her red Honda Accord:** "Victim Describes Crash into Plasma Center," News 4 broadcast, October 30, 2014, https://www.news4jax.com/news/2014/10/30/victim -describes-crash-into-plasma-center/

26 **from writer Darryl Lorenzo Wellington:** Darryl Lorenzo Wellington, "The Twisted Business of Donating Plasma," *Atlantic*, May 2014, https://www.theatlantic.com/health /archive/2014/05/blood-money-the-twisted-business-of-do nating-plasma/362012/

26 **So much of the world's blood plasma comes:** Nicola Lacetera, Mario Macis, and Robert Slonim, "Economic Rewards

to Motivate Blood Donations," *Science*, May 24, 2013, https://www.science.org/doi/abs/10.1126/science.1232280. Also, Neelam Dhingra, "In Defense of the WHO's Blood Donation Policy," *Science*, November 8, 2013, https://www.science.org/doi/10.1126/science.342.6159.691

27 **A substantial portion of the blood plasma:** J. Prevot and S. Jolles, "Global Immunoglobulin Supply: Steaming Towards the Iceberg?," *Current Opinion in Allergy and Clinical Immunology* 20, no. 6 (December 2020): 557–64, https://doi.org/10.1097/ACI.0000000000000696. PMID: 33044340; PMCID: PMC7752222.

27 **United States the "OPEC of Plasma":** Rose George, *Nine Pints: A Journey Through the Money, Medicine, and Mysteries of Blood* (New York: Macmillan, 2018).

27 **comparable to a global oil cartel:** Sylvie Douglis, "Blood Money," *Planet Money*, NPR broadcast, May 14, 2021, https://www.npr.org/transcripts/996921658

27 **flows into global medicines:** Douglas Starr, *Blood: An Epic History of Medicine and Commerce* (New York: Alfred A. Knopf, 1998).

27 **cutthroat capitalism that powers:** Zoe Greenburg, "What Is the Blood of a Poor Person Worth?," *New York Times*, February 1, 2019, https://www.nytimes.com/2019/02/01/sunday-review/blood-plasma-industry.html

29 **nearly one-third of American workers earn:** "The Crisis of Low Wages in the US," Oxfam America, March 21, 2022, https://www.oxfamamerica.org/explore/research-publications/the-crisis-of-low-wages-in-the-us/

30 **Years of economic studies have shown:** "New Data Illustrate the Failure of the Trickle Down Experiment," Center for American Progress, 2015, https://www.americanprogress.org/article/new-data-illustrate-the-failure-of-the-trickle-down-experiment/2015

31 **"We don't really know why it works":** Claire Larroche et al., "Mechanisms of Intravenous Immunoglobulin Action in the Treatment of Autoimmune Disorders," *BioDrugs* 16, no. 1 (2002): 47–55, https://doi.org/10.2165/00063030-200216010-00005

37 **Luke Shaefer, director:** Analidis Ochoa and Luke Shaefer, "The Interlinkage Between Blood Plasma Donation and Poverty," report, February 2021, University of Michigan Poverty Solutions, http://sites.fordschool.umich.edu/poverty2021/files/2021/05 /The-Interlinkage-between-Blood-Plasma-Donation-and-Pov erty-February-2021.pdf

37 **Shaefer and Edin reached:** Kathryn J. Edin and Luke Shaefer, *$2.00 a Day: Living on Almost Nothing in America* (Boston: Houghton Mifflin Harcourt, 2015). Also, Kathryn J. Edin and Luke Shaefer, "Blood Plasma, Sweat, and Tears," *Atlantic*, September 1, 2015, https://www.theatlantic.com/business/archive /2015/09/poor-sell-blood/403012/

39 **more than 1,000 by 2021:** *CSL Plasma Inc. et al. v. U.S. Customs and Border Protection*, Civil Action No. 1:21-cv-2360 (United States District Court for the District of Columbia), filed September 7, 2021, https://www.courthousenews.com/wp-content /uploads/2022/05/csl-plasma-complaint.pdf

40 **A local newspaper story:** Tyler Christensen, "Biolife/Easy Profits," *Missoulian*, October 20, 2006, https://missoulian.com /news/biolife-easy-profits/article_2f26ce6f-e12d-52e1-be15 -36235e893c6c.html

41 **From Dallas, Texas, to Spokane:** "Blood Money," *Inlander*, October 21, 2009, https://www.inlander.com/spokane/blood -money/Content?oid=2130052

41 **to Joplin, Kansas:** Rich Brown, "Plasma Donors Helping Others," *Joplin Globe*, October 18, 2006, https://www.joplinglobe .com/news/lifestyles/plasma-donors-helping-others/article _d0ca7d4e-2d24-5270-8ae2-6830f4ae4c4d.html

CHAPTER 3: Mormon Country, U.S.A.

45 **The most interesting event:** Associated Press, "Paper Gets Records Detailing Remote Idaho Shootout," *Argus Observer*, September 3, 2012, https://www.argusobserver.com/news/paper-gets-records -detailing-remote-idaho-shootout/article_52e86d02-f6ca-5beb -a539-cb0dfa348a6c.html

45 **ever more gentrified:** Carter Williams, "Outdoor Recreation Created $5.5B in Utah: Here's How That Stacks Up with Other

States," KSL-TV broadcast, September 2019, https://www.ksl
.com/article/46642324/outdoor-recreation-created-55b-in
-utah-heres-how-that-stacks-up-with-other-states. Also, Justin
Farrell, *Billionaire Wilderness: The Ultra-Wealthy and the Re-
making of the American West* (Princeton, NJ: Princeton University Press, 2020).

47 **One of the first people I talked with:** Rett Nelson, telephone
interviews with author, various times in 2021.

48 **A plasma donation does take longer than a blood donation:**
Elizabeth Preston, "Why You Get Paid to Donate Plasma but
Not Blood," *STAT News*, January 22, 2016, https://www.stat
news.com/2016/01/22/paid-plasma-not-blood/

49 **A woman named Lori Vallow:** Leah Sottile, *When the Moon
Turns to Blood: Lori Vallow, Chad Daybell, and a Story of Murder, Wild Faith, and End Times* (New York: Twelve Books, 2022).

55 **In a 2010 study, researchers:** R. Laub, S. Baurin, D. Timmer-
man, T. Branckaert, and P. Strengers, "Specific Protein Content
of Pools of Plasma for Fractionation from Different Sources: Impact of Frequency of Donations," *Vox Sanguinis* 99, no. 3 (2010):
220–31, https://doi.org/10.1111/j.1423-0410.2010.01345.x

55 **the health of 6,000 plasma donors in China:** Xi Chen, "Commercial Plasma Donation and Individual Health in Impover-
ished Rural China," *Health Economics Review* 4, no. 30 (2014):
[n.p.], https://doi.org/10.1186/s13561-014-0030-6.

CHAPTER 4: The Blood of Our Youth

57 **BYU-Idaho is deeply troubled:** Bill Chappell, "College Says
Students May Have Sought COVID-19 Infection to Boost
Plasma Donor Payout," NPR broadcast, October 13, 2020,
https://www.npr.org/sections/coronavirus-live-updates
/2020/10/13/923381540/college-says-students-may-have-sou
ght-covid-19-infection-to-boost-plasma-donor-p

57 **"BYU-Idaho recognizes that":** Courtney Tanner, "BYU-Idaho
Says Students May Be Trying to Get COVID-19 so They Can
Sell Their Plasma," *Salt Lake Tribune*, October 13, 2020, https://
www.sltrib.com/news/education/2020/10/13/byu-idaho-says
-students/

58 **multiple national news stories:** Chappell, "College Says Students."

58 **people who remained unvaccinated:** Lindsay Monte, "Household Pulse Survey Shows Many Don't Trust Covid Vaccine," United States Census Bureau, December, 28, 2021, https://www .census.gov/library/stories/2021/12/who-are-the-adults-not -vaccinated-against-covid

60 **German scientist Emil Adolf von Behring:** "Emil von Behring: The Founder of Serum Therapy," Nobel Prize, December 3, 2001, https://www.nobelprize.org/prizes/medicine/1901/beh ring/article/

60 **A 2006 meta-study of patients:** T. C. Luke, E. M. Kilbane, J. L. Jackson, and S. L. Hoffman, "Meta-Analysis: Convalescent Blood Products for Spanish Influenza Pneumonia: A Future H5N1 Treatment?" *Annals of Internal Medicine* 145, no. 8 (October 17, 2006): 599–609, https://doi.org/10.7326/0003-4819-145-8 -200610170-00139. Epub 2006 Aug 29. PMID: 16940336

61 **the plasma of people who had been infected with:** "An Update on Convalescent Plasma for COVID-19," Bloomberg School of Public Health, Johns Hopkins University, January 18, 2022, https://publichealth.jhu.edu/2022/an-update-on-convalescent -plasma-for-covid-19

61 **The plasma was used in research:** "A Randomized Trial of Convalescent Plasma in Covid-19 Severe Pneumonia," *New England Journal of Medicine*, February 18, 2022, [n.p.], https://www .nejm.org/doi/full/10.1056/nejmoa2031304

61 **the grand experiment . . . had flopped:** Cormac Sheridan, "Convalescent Plasma Falls Flat in First Randomized Trial," *Nature*, September 24, 2020, https://www.nature.com/articles/d41587 -020-00020-0

61 **"There was no clear benefit":** "WHO Recommends Against the Use of Convalescent Plasma to Treat COVID-19," World Health Organization, December 7, 2021, https://www.who.int /news/item/07-12-2021-who-recommends-against-the-use-of -convalescent-plasma-to-treat-covid-19

61 **a well-connected Republican political donor:** Associated Press, "Trump Admin Funds Plasma Company Based in Owner's Condo," November 1, 2020, https://www.pbs.org/newshour/na

tion/trump-admin-funds-plasma-company-based-in-owners
-condo

62 **It had done next to nothing:** "NIH Study Shows No Significant Benefit of Convalescent Plasma for COVID-19 Outpatients with Early Symptoms," National Institutes of Health,
August 18, 2021, https://www.nih.gov/news-events/news-re
leases/nih-study-shows-no-significant-benefit-convales
cent-plasma-covid-19-outpatients-early-symptoms

62 **findings reported in the** *New England Journal*: "NIH Study
Shows No Significant Benefit of Convalescent Plasma for
COVID-19 Outpatients with Early Symptoms," National Institutes of Health, August 18, 2021, https://www.nih.gov
/news-events/news-releases/nih-study-shows-no-significant
-benefit-convalescent-plasma-covid-19-outpatients-early
-symptoms#:~:text=%E2%80%9CWe%20were%20hoping%20
that%20the,Clifton%20Callaway%2C%20M.D.%2C%20Ph

63 **it's expensive to live in Idaho:** Benjamin Enggas, "Housing
Shortages Plague Individuals, Families Looking to Rent in
Rexburg," *Rexburg Standard Journal*, August 30, 2021, https://
www.rexburgstandardjournal.com/news/local/housing-short
ages-plague-individuals-families-looking-to-rent-in-rexburg
/article_198ee712-ded6-5a56-abb6-aa031fcffb2a.html

64 **according to the Education Data Initiative:** Melanie Hanson,
"Average Cost of College and Tuition," Education Data Initiative,
August 15, 2022, https://educationdata.org/average-cost-of-col
lege

65 **the reasons women sell their eggs:** Diane Tober, "Student
Debt Is Driving More Americans to Donate Their Eggs and
Some Suffer Lasting Complications," *Salon*, February 14, 2021,
https://www.salon.com/2021/02/14/student-debt-is-driving
-more-americans-to-donate-their-eggs--and-some-suffer-last
ing-complications/

65 **"The United States emerges":** Tober, "Student Debt."

CHAPTER 5: Moving Blood

72 *Transfusio de sang du chèvre*: Mark Roth, "1892 Painting Il-
lustrates Odd Links Among Animals, Art & Medicine," *Pitts-*

burgh Post-Gazette, May 8, 2006, https://www.post-gazette.com
/news/health/2006/05/08/1892-painting-illustrates-odd-links
-among-animals-art-medicine/stories/200605080210

73   **The history of medicine is riddled:** Holly Tucker, *Blood Work:
A Tale of Medicine and Murder in the Scientific Revolution* (New
York: W. W. Norton, 2012).

73   **devouring the blood of the young:** David Robson, "The People Who Drink Human Blood," BBC, https://www.bbc.com/fu
ture/article/20151021-the-people-who-drink-human-blood

73   **Pope Innocent VIII:** Jeremy Cohen, "Pope Innocent III, Chris-
tian Wet Nurses, and Jews," *Jewish Quarterly Review* 107, no. 1
(Winter 2017): 113–28, https://www.jstor.org/stable/90000707

73   **advances in blood science by London's Royal Society:** Bill
Hayes, *Five Quarts: A Personal and Natural History of Blood*
(New York: Random House, 2005).

74   **Alexander Bogdanov in Russia:** Douglas Huestis, "Alexander
Bogdanov: The Forgotten Pioneer of Blood Transfusion," *Transfusion Medicine Reviews*, October 2007, https://www.science
direct.com/science/article/abs/pii/S0887796307000478

74   **Bloody tales throughout human history:** Natalie Coleman,
"Out for Young Blood," *Nautilus*, September 25, 2017, https://
nautil.us/out-for-young-blood-6634/

74   **blood as a fountain of youth:** Sabrina Maddeaux, "Why the
Wealthy Believe the Fountain of Youth Flows with Blood, and Are
Spending Thousands to Satiate Their Lust," *National Post*, September 27, 2016, https://nationalpost.com/life/fashion-beauty
/why-the-wealthy-believe-the-fountain-of-youth-flows-with
-blood-and-are-spending-thousands-to-satiate-their-lust

74   **a British doctor kept dogs alive:** Elizabeth Yale, "First Blood
Transfusion: A History," JSTOR Daily, April 22, 2015, https://
daily.jstor.org/first-blood-transfusion/

75   **fractionation machine:** "Charles Richard Drew: Father of the
Blood Bank," American Chemical Society, [n.d.], https://www
.acs.org/content/acs/en/education/whatischemistry/african
-americans-in-sciences/charles-richard-drew.html

75   **A doctor named Ogden Carr Bruton:** S. Ponader and J. A.
Burger, "Bruton's Tyrosine Kinase: From X-linked Agamma-
globulinemia Toward Targeted Therapy for B-cell Malignan-

cies," *Journal of Clinical Oncology* 32, no. 17 (2014): 1830–39, https://doi.org/10.1200/JCO.2013.53.1046

76 **plasma industry has also described research:** *CSL Plasma Inc., et al. v. U.S. Customs and Border Protection*, Civil Action No. 1:21-cv-2360 (United States District Court for the District of Columbia), filed September 7, 2021, https://www.courthousenews .com/wp-content/uploads/2022/05/csl-plasma-complaint.pdf

CHAPTER 6: The Vampires of Capitalism

82 **introduce into humans:** Bruce Goldman, "Infusion of Young Blood Recharges Brains of Old Mice, Study Finds," Stanford Medicine News Center, May 4, 2014, https://med.stanford.edu /news/all-news/2014/05/infusion-of-young-blood-recharges -brains-of-old-mice-study-finds.html

82 **reverse the aging process:** Alok Jha, "Young Blood Can Reverse Some Effects of Ageing, Study Finds," *Guardian*, October 17, 2012, https://www.theguardian.com/science/2012/oct/17 /young-blood-reverse-effects-ageing?cat=science&type=arti cle

82 **reverse some of the markers of aging:** Ian Samples, "Can We Reverse the Ageing Process by Putting Young Blood into Older People?," *Guardian*, August 4, 2015, https://www.theguardian .com/science/2015/aug/04/can-we-reverse-ageing-process -young-blood-older-people

82 **might be different this time:** Jocelyn Kaiser, "Young Blood Renews Old Mice," *Science*, May 14, 2014, [n.p.]. Also, Jocelyn Kaiser, "Young Blood Anti-Aging Trial Raises Questions," *Science*, August 1, 2016, https://www.science.org/content/article /young-blood-antiaging-trial-raises-questions

82 **Villeda's team stitched the animals' arteries:** Samples, "Can We Reverse."

83 **animals in the California experiments:** B. Hofmann, "Young Blood Rejuvenates Old Bodies: A Call for Reflection When Moving from Mice to Men," *Transfusion Medicine Hemotherapy* 45, no. 1 (2018): 67–71, https://doi.org/10.1159/000481828

83 **"giving young blood":** Alok Jah, "Young Blood Reverses Some Effects of Ageing, Study Finds."

84 **not part of the Stanford lab trials:** Jesse Karmazin, "Ambrosia Plasma Relaunches," Live Forever Club, February 3, 2020, https://liveforever.club/blog/ambrosia-plasma-relaunches-announces-improvement-in-key-ageing-biomarkers

84 **the high-pitched buzz:** Tanya Basu and Kelly Weill, "FDA Warns: Don't Give These Companies Your 'Young Blood,'" *Daily Beast*, February 22, 2019, https://www.thedailybeast.com/fda-warns-dont-giv-these-companie-your-young-blood

87 **"The Food and Drug Administration (FDA) is advising":** Rebecca Robbins, "FDA Issues Warning About Young Blood Transfusions," *STAT News*, February 20, 2019, https://www.scientific american.com/article/fda-issues-warning-about-young-blood-transfusions/

CHAPTER 7: Vanity and Blood

90 **made famous by celebrities like Kim Kardashian:** Macaela Mackenzie, "Kim Kardashian West Regrets Getting Her Infamous Vampire Facial," *Allure*, March 1, 2018, https://www.allure .com/story/kim-kardashian-west-regrets-vampire-facial

90 **"Then the ghost of Theban Teiresias":** Homer, *The Odyssey* (London/New York: W. Heinemann/G. P. Putnam, 1919).

91 **The "Summer of *Morbius*":** Kirsten Mettler, "'Morbius' Sucks: Meet the Sony/Marvel Vampire Flop," *Stanford Daily*, April 6, 2022, https://stanforddaily.com/2022/04/06/morbius-sucks-meet -the-sony-marvel-vampire-flop/

CHAPTER 8: Hollowed Out and Never Enough

99 **fallen by 26 percent:** Mason Walker, "U.S. Newsroom Employment Has Fallen 26% Since 2008," Pew Research Center, July 13, 2021, https://www.pewresearch.org/fact-tank/2021/07/13/u-s -newsroom-employment-has-fallen-26-since-2008/

99 **the building sold to developers:** Katie Miller, "Missoulian Building Sells, Developers Announce Plans," KPAX-TV broadcast, November 26, 2021, https://www.kpax.com/news /missoula-county/missoulian-building-sells-developers-announce-plans

99 **places that no longer have a local newspaper:** Penny Muse Abernathy, "The Expanding News Desert," 2020 report for the University of North Carolina, https://www.usnewsdeserts.com

CHAPTER 9: The Rust in Our Veins

115 **assassination of a newspaper owner and editor in Nicaragua:** Alan Riding, "New Rioting Erupts in Nicaragua Capital," *New York Times*, January 13, 1978, https://www.nytimes.com/1978/01/13/archives/new-jersey-pages-new-rioting-erupts-in-nicaragua-capital-protesters.html

115 **Journalist Pedro Joaquín Chamorro:** Susan Meiselas, "National Mutiny in Nicaragua," *New York Times*, July 30, 1978, https://www.nytimes.com/1978/07/30/archives/national-mutiny-in-nicaragua-nicaragua.html

116 **Americans supplying two-thirds of the world's plasma:** "An Analysis of the Impact of International Transfers of Plasma," report by PPTA Global, https://www.pptaglobal.org/images/source/2019/Fall/An_Analysis_of_the_Impact_of_International_Transfers_of_Plasma_on_the_Availability_of_Immunoglobulin_Therapies.pdf

CHAPTER 10: Flint

121 **"Sit down! Sit down!":** Timothy P. Lynch, " 'Sit Down! Sit Down!': Songs of the General Motors Strike, 1936–1937," *Michigan Historical Review* 22, no. 2 (1996): 1–47, https://doi.org/10.2307/20173585

121 **nickname dates back to the city's:** Emily Bingham, "Michigan History: Why Flint's Vehicle City Has Nothing to Do with Cars," MLive, May 25, 2017, https://www.mlive.com/entertainment/2017/05/flint_vehicle_city_name_history.html

122 **Management tried to argue:** "Sit-Down Men and Stand-Up Women," Roadside America, https://www.roadsideamerica.com/story/23099

122 **The Flint Sit-Down Strike:** Edward McLelland, *Midnight in Vehicle City: General Motors, Flint, and the Strike That Created the Middle Class* (Boston: Beacon Press, 2021).

123 **better wages and factory working conditions:** Sidney Fine, *Sit-Down: The General Motors Strike of 1936–1937* (Ann Arbor: University of Michigan Press, 2020).

123 **In oral histories preserved:** The Flint Sit-Down Strike Audio Gallery, Michigan State University, http://flint.matrix.msu .edu

123 **labor practices of contemporary American life at companies like Amazon:** E. Tammy Kim, "How to Unionize at Amazon," *New Yorker*, April 7, 2022, https://www.newyorker.com/news /dispatch/how-to-unionize-at-amazon

123 **copper miners in the 1910s and 1920s:** Nate Schweber, "In Butte, Remembering the Fallen—but Not One Who Stood Up," *Parts Unknown*, April 4, 2017, https://explorepartsunknown .com/montana/butte-mining-unions/

124 **the film *Roger & Me*:** *Roger & Me*, documentary film written and directed by Michael Moore, Dog Eat Dog Films, 1989.

124 **Many families left the city:** *The Poisoning of an American City*, documentary film, written and directed by David Barnhart, 2019.

124 **industrial abandonment is a staggering poverty rate:** Dominic Adams, "Here's How Flint Went from Boomtown to Nation's Highest Poverty Rate," MLive, September 21, 2017, https:// www.mlive.com/news/flint/2017/09/heres_how_flint_went _from_boom.html

131 **poisoned by lead in their water:** Anna Clark, *The Poisoned City: Flint's Water and the American Urban Tragedy* (New York: Metropolitan Books, 2018).

CHAPTER 11: The Father of Blood Banking

133 **retraced his life:** Charles B. Drew, "Stranger Than Fact," *New York Times*, April 7, 1996, https://www.nytimes.com/1996/04/07 /books/stranger-than-fact.html

133 **historian Spencie Love:** Spencie Love, *One Blood: The Death and Resurrection of Charles R. Drew* (Chapel Hill: University of North Carolina Press, 1996).

135 **his daughter Charlene Drew Jarvis recalled:** Kamilah Kashanie, "Remembering the Father of Blood Banking, a Black Doctor

Who Took a Stand," NPR broadcast, August 25, 2021, https://www.npr.org/2021/08/06/1025372235/pioneer-charles-drew-blood-plasma-preservation-red-cross

135 **"It happened one April day while":** North Caroline Museum of History, "The Death of Charles Drew," https://www.ncmuseumofhistory.org/death-dr-charles-drew

136 **Cornelia Spencer "Spencie" Love:** Love, *One Blood.*

CHAPTER 12: Crime, Punishment, and Plasma

139 **petty infractions like traffic tickets:** Spencer S. Hsu, "Jennings to Pay $4.7 Million Settlement to Those Jailed over Court Debts," *Washington Post*, July 14, 2016, https://www.stltoday.com/news/local/metro/jennings-to-pay-4-7m-settlement-to-those-jailed-over-court-debts/article_e0ffdc5c-6996-5cb9-b9db-8d6cbfa9dc0a.html

139 **issued more warrants than the number of households:** Campbell Robertson, "Missouri City to Pay $4.7 Million to Settle Suit over Jailing Practices," *New York Times*, July 15, 2016, https://www.nytimes.com/2016/07/16/us/missouri-city-to-pay-4-7-million-to-settle-suit-over-jailing-practices.html

139 **de facto ending of cash bail:** "The Case for Ending Cash Bail," Bail Project, April 2012, https://bailproject.org/after-cash-bail/

142 **an especially egregious case in Alabama:** Campbell Robertson, "For Offenders Who Can't Pay, It's a Pint of Blood or Jail Time," *New York Times*, October 19, 2015, https://www.nytimes.com/2015/10/20/us/for-offenders-who-cant-pay-its-a-pint-of-blood-or-jail-time.html

142 **longtime circuit court judge:** Court of the Judiciary, Alabama, In the Matter of Marvin Wiggins, https://judicial.alabama.gov/docs/judiciary/COJ51WigginsAmended.pdf

142 **show up with receipts for blood donations:** Stephanie Taylor, "Judge Marvin Wiggins Under Investigation for Fourth Time in 10 Years," *Tuscaloosa News*, December 4, 2019, https://www.tuscaloosanews.com/story/news/2019/12/04/judge-marvin-wiggins-under-investigation-for-fourth-time-in-10-years/2151325007/

142 **judge didn't push people directly:** Kent Faulk, "Judge Who

Demanded Blood from Defendants Charged, Suspended," AL.com, January 16, 2016, https://www.al.com/news/birming ham/2016/01/alabama_blood_or_jail_judge_su.html

143 **coffers of the Arkansas correctional system:** Suzi Parker, "Blood Money," *Salon*, November 30, 1998, https://www.salon .com/1998/11/30/news950556562/

144 **no other place has gone bigger:** Sophia Chase, "The Bloody Truth," *William and Mary Business Law Review* [n.v., n.d.], https://scholarship.law.wm.edu/cgi/viewcontent.cgi?article =1042&context=wmblr

144 **"After passing a few blood tests":** Mara Leveritt, "Blood Money," *Arkansas Times*, March 1991, https://arktimes.com/news/cover -stories/2004/09/23/1991-blood-money.

145 **the FDA ordered American drugmakers:** "Poison from the Prisons," *Economist*, March 11, 1999, https://www.econo mist.com/united-states/1999/03/11/poison-from-the-prisons

145 **thousands of Americans had contracted the virus:** US Institute of Medicine Committee to Study HIV Transmission through Blood and Blood Products, "HIV and the Blood Supply: An Analysis of Crisis Decisionmaking," ed. Lauren B. Leveton, Harold C. Sox Jr., and Michael A Stoto (Washington, DC: National Academies Press, 1995).

145 **Bayer had paid out millions to settle:** L. McHenry, and M. Khosh-nood, "Blood Money: Bayer's Inventory of HIV-Contaminated Blood Products and Third World Hemophiliacs," Account res-olution, *PubMed* 21, no. 6 (2014): 389–400, https://doi.org/10.1 080/08989621.2014.882780. PMID: 24785997, https://pubmed .ncbi.nlm.nih.gov/24785997/. See also https://www.theguardian .com/world/2003/may/23/aids.suzannegoldenberg

146 **A Canadian government investigation:** Sophia Chase, "The Bloody Truth: Examining America's Blood Industry." *William and Mary Law Review*, April 2012, https://scholarship.law .wm.edu/cgi/viewcontent.cgi?article=1042&context=wmblr

146 **Ryuhei Kawada has been diagnosed:** Tim Healy and Murakami Mutsuko, "Profiles in Courage," *Asiaweek*, Novem-ber 30, 2000.

147 **he rubbed the back of one hand:** Ryuhei Kawada, interview with author, September 2015, Tokyo.

147 **Kawada joined a lawsuit against his country's:** Masami Ito, "Clock Ticking as Counselor Kawada Goes After What Has Long Ailed Japan," *Japan Times*, September 5, 2007, https://www .japantimes.co.jp/news/2007/09/05/national/clock-ticking-as -councilor-kawada-goes-after-what-has-long-ailed-japan/

CHAPTER 13: Borderlands

151 **most reliable streams of blood sellers:** Dara Lind, "The US Is Closing a Loophole That Lured Mexicans Across the Border to Donate Blood Plasma for Cash," ProPublica, June 24, 2021, https://www.propublica.org/article/the-us-is-closing-a-loop hole-that-lured-mexicans-over-the-border-to-donate-blood -plasma-for-cash

155 **2019 investigative report from ProPublica:** Stefanie Dodt and Lucas Strozyk, "Pharmaceutical Companies Are Luring Mexicans Across the U.S. Border to Donate Blood Plasma," ProPublica/ARD German Television, October 4, 2019, https://www .propublica.org/article/pharmaceutical-companies-are-luring -mexicans-across-the-u.s.-border-to-donate-blood-plasma

155 **10,000 Mexican citizens:** Dodt and Strozyk, "Pharmaceutical Companies."

156 **closures led, in part, to a months-long shortage:** Keith Romer, "Another Shortage Caused by the Pandemic: Blood Plasma," NPR broadcast, May 21, 2021, https://www.npr .org/2021/05/21/999241523/another-shortage-caused-by-the -pandemic-blood-plasma

158 **accepted practice for thirty years:** *CSL Plasma Inc. et al. v. U.S. Customs and Border Protection*, Civil Action No. 1:21-cv-2360 (United States District Court for the District of Columbia), filed September 7, 2021, https://www.courthousenews.com/wp-con tent/uploads/2022/05/csl-plasma-complaint.pdf

CHAPTER 14: A Battle for Blood on the Border

162 **illogical partial closure:** Carolina Cuellar, "We Don't Know How We're Going to Survive," Texas Public Radio broadcast, June 16, 2021, https://www.tpr.org/border-immigration/2021-06-16

/headline-we-dont-know-how-were-going-to-survive-many
-mexican-nationals-can-no-longer-cross-the-border-to-sell
-their-blood-plasma

162 **52 border blood plasma centers:** *CSL Plasma Inc. et al. v. U.S. Customs and Border Protection*, Civil Action No. 1:21-cv-2360 (United States District Court for the District of Columbia), filed September 7, 2021, https://www.courthousenews.com/wp-con tent/uploads/2022/05/csl-plasma-complaint.pdf

163 **"Selling plasma constitutes labor for hire":** *CSL Plasma Inc. et al. v. U.S. Customs and Border Protection.*

163 **most productive in the country:** *CSL Plasma Inc. et al. v. U.S. Customs and Border Protection.*

164 **plasma is a paradigmatic example:** *CSL Plasma Inc. et al. v. U.S. Customs and Border Protection.*

165 **United States is the OPEC of blood plasma:** Gilbert Gaul, "America: The OPEC of the Global Plasma Industry," *Philadelphia Inquirer*, March 12, 2009, https://www.inquirer.com/philly/on line_extras/America_the_opec_of_the_global_plasma_industry .html

166 **industry that targets disparity only where it can:** Analidis Ochoa and Luke Shaefer, "How Blood Plasma Companies Target the Poorest Americans," *Atlantic*, March 15, 2018, https:// www.theatlantic.com/business/archive/2018/03/plasma-dona tions/555599/

166 **Mexican donors cannot get paid for their plasma:** Mark Cherney, Renee Onque, and Daniela Hernandez, "Block on Blood-Plasma Donors from Mexico Threatens Supplies," *Wall Street Journal*, March 9, 2022, https://www.wsj.com/articles/block-on-blood -plasma-donors-from-mexico-threatens-supplies-11646830295

166 **donations were down by 20 percent:** "Plasma Donations Remain Disappointingly Low Through Ongoing Pandemic, Risking Patients' Lives," Plasma Protein Therapeutics Association, https:// www.pptaglobal.org/media-and-information/157-media -and-information/ppta-statements/1119-plasma-donations-re main-disappointingly-low-through-ongoing-pandemic-risk ing-patients-lives

166 **ruled in favor of the plasma companies:** *CSL Plasma Inc. et al. v. U.S. Customs and Border Protection*, Ruling No.

21-5282, May 10, 2022, https://www.cadc.uscourts.gov /internet/opinions.nsf/9C923DB1DAEC91048525883E004FB 4B0/$file/21-5282-1946110.pdf

167 **Member Code of Ethics:** Plasma Protein Therapy Association, [n.d.], https://www.pptaglobal.org/media-and-information/18 -membership/52-code-of-ethics

CHAPTER 15: The Blood Givers' Union

171 **the 1930s in New York City:** Blood Transfusion Betterment Association, *Bulletin of the New York Academy of Medicine* 6, no. 10 (October 1930): 682–87, PMID: 19311751; PMCID: PMC2096130, https://www.ncbi.nlm.nih.gov/pmc/articles/ PMC2096130/?page=1

171 **recognized labor union in 1938:** "Blood Givers' Form a Union," *New York Times*, September 15, 1938, https://timesmachine .nytimes.com/timesmachine/1938/09/15/96837879.html?page Number=27

171 **Blood Transfusion Betterment Association:** D. W. Stetten, "The Blood Transfusion Betterment Association of New York City: Organization and Functioning of the Association and Its Blood Donor Bureau," *JAMA* 110, no. 16 (1938): 1248–52, https://doi .org/10.1001/jama.1938.02790160006002

172 **by no fault of their own:** Blood Transfusion Betterment Association, *Bulletin*, 3.

172 **The donors, unhappy with their pay cut:** Susan E. Lederer, *Flesh and Blood: Organ Transplantation and Blood Transfusion in 20th Century America* (London: Oxford University Press, 2008), 88.

172 **relying on person-to-person transmission:** Spencie Love, *One Blood: The Death and Resurrection of Charles R. Drew* (Chapel Hill: University of North Carolina Press, 1996).

173 **"He did not disclose what might happen:** "Blood Givers' Form a Union."

174 **Support for labor unions has grown:** Justin McCarthy, "U.S. Approval of Labor Unions at Highest Point Since 1965," Gallup, August 30, 2022, https://news.gallup.com/poll/398303/approval -labor-unions-highest-point-1965.aspx

175 **efforts at facilities of major businesses:** Noam Scheiber, "REI Workers in New York Vote to Unionize," *New York Times*, March 3, 2022, https://www.nytimes.com/2022/03/02/business /rei-union-new-york.html

175 **successfully unionized in March 2022:** Andrea Hsu, "Starbucks Workers Drive Nationwide Surge in Union Organizing," NPR broadcast, May 1, 2022, https://www.npr.org /2022/05/01/1095477792/union-election-labor-starbucks -workers-food-service-representation

175 **This modern era of renewed interest in union organizing:** Jodi Kantor and Karen Weise, "Amazon vs. the Union," *New York Times*, April 4, 2015, https://www.nytimes.com/2022/04/15 /briefing/amazon-union-warehouse.html

CHAPTER 16: What to Do About the Giant Pool

178 **its true impact remains covered up:** Gao Yaojie, *The Soul of Gao Yaojie* (Hong Kong: Ming Pao Publications, 2017).

179 **centers prey on the precarity:** Kathryn J. Edin and Luke Shaefer, "Blood Plasma, Sweat, and Tears," *Atlantic*, September 1, 2015, https://www.theatlantic.com/business/archive/2015/09/poor -sell-blood/403012/

182 **why are we the only country:** Sylvie Douglis, "Blood Money," *Planet Money*, NPR broadcast, May 14, 2021, https://www.npr .org/transcripts/996921658

182 **fixing American capitalism:** Analidis Ochoa and Luke Shaefer, "How Blood Plasma Companies Target the Poorest Americans," *Atlantic*, March 15, 2018, https://www.theatlantic.com/busi ness/archive/2018/03/plasma-donations/555599/

EPILOGUE

185 **Anne Hunsaker Hawkins:** Anne Hunsaker Hawkins, *Reconstructing Illness* (South Bend, IN: Purdue University Press, 1999).

185 **private tragedies and hardship:** Susan Sontag, *Illness as a Metaphor* (New York: Farrar, Straus & Giroux, 1978).

186 **According to a Lugar Center statement:** "Richard Lugar, Long-

time Senator and Foreign Policy Sage, Has Died at 87," CBS News broadcast, April 28, 2019, https://www.cbsnews.com /news/richard-lugar-died-former-senator-foreign-policy-expert -dead-age-87-cause-of-death-2019-04-28/

187 **"something of a medical mystery":** Adam Dudding, "Paul Fue-mana's Rare Disease Revealed," *Stuff*, April 25, 2010, https:// www.stuff.co.nz/national/3620282/Pauly-Fuemanas-rare-dis ease-revealed

187 **The author of *Catch-22*:** Joseph Heller and Speed Vogel, *No Laughing Matter* (Ann Arbor: University of Michigan Press, 1986).

187 **Heller died of a heart attack:** Sarah Manguso, *The Two Kinds of Decay* (New York: Picador Press, 2008).

INDEX

ABOUT THE AUTHOR

Kathleen McLaughlin is an award-winning journalist who reports and writes about the consequences of economic inequality around the world. A frequent contributor to the *Washington Post* and the *Guardian,* McLaughlin's reporting has also appeared in the *New York Times, BuzzFeed,* the *Atlantic,* the *Economist,* on NPR, and more. She is a former Knight Science Journalism fellow at MIT and has won multiple awards for her reporting on labor in China. *Blood Money* is her first book.